Protecting Free Trade

The author (left) with Sir David Trench, Governor of Hong Kong, 1964–71

Protecting Free Trade

The Hong Kong Paradox, 1947–97

A Personal Reminiscence

Lawrence W. R. Mills

香港大學出版社
HONG KONG UNIVERSITY PRESS

Hong Kong University Press
14/F Hing Wai Centre
7 Tin Wan Praya Road
Aberdeen
Hong Kong
www.hkupress.org

ISBN 978-988-8083-98-5

British Library Cataloguing-in-Publication Data
A catalogue record for this book is available from the British Library.

10 9 8 7 6 5 .4 3 2 1

Printed and bound by Liang Yu Printing Factory Ltd., in Hong Kong, China

Contents

Abbreviations

ACP	African Caribbean Pacific (states party to a trade agreement with the EEC, q.v.)
ADC	Aide-de-Camp
AO	Administrative Officer
ASEAN	Association of Southeast Asian Nations
ATO	Assistant Trade Officer, the first level of the Trade Officer Grade
B.C.C.	British Crown Colony
BOAC	British Overseas Airways Corporation
CAB	Cotton Advisory Board
CCO	Combined Certificate of Origin (for the USA, q.v.)
CHKO	Certificate of Hong Kong Origin, certifying that a product was genuinely manufactured in Hong Kong. A CO, q.v., merely certified origin by reference to supporting documents
CIA	Central Intelligence Agency
CO	Certificate of Origin; Clerical Officer
COMITEXTIL	Coordination Committee for the Textile Industries in the European Economic Community
CPC	Commonwealth Preference Certificate
DC&I	The abbreviation widely used in Hong Kong for the Commerce and Industry Department of the Hong Kong government
DG	Director General (of the GATT, q.v.)
D-TIC	Director of Trade, Industry and Customs
EC	European Community
EEC	European Economic Community
EFTA	European Free Trade Area

E/A	(Textiles) Export Authorisation
E/L	(Textiles) Export Licence
EO	Executive Officer
EXCO	Executive Council (of the Hong Kong government)
FAC	Foreign Assets Control
FCO	Foreign and Commonwealth Office (of the UK, q.v., government)
FS	Financial Secretary
GACOS	Government Approved Certificate of Origin Suppliers
GATT	General Agreement on Tariffs and Trade
GDP	Gross Domestic Product
GSP	Generalised Scheme of Preferences
HCCS	High Cost Content Scheme
HKTDC	Hong Kong Trade Development Council
ICAC	Independent Commission Against Corruption
ILO	International Labour Organisation
ITO	International Trade Organisation
LDC	Less developed country, the now not-politically-correct shorthand for developing countries
LEGCO	Legislative Council (of the Hong Kong government)
LTA	Long-Term Arrangement Regarding International Trade in Cotton Textiles
MBE	Member of the Order of the British Empire
MFA	Multi-fibre Arrangement, the widely used name for the Arrangement Regarding International Trade in Textiles
MFN	most-favoured-nation (Article I of the GATT, q.v.)
mmf	man-made fibres
MP	Member of Parliament
MVP	minimum viable production, the 'Nordic' clause in the MFA, q.v.
NIC	Newly Industrialised/Industrialising Country
PD	Police Department
PHQ	Police Headquarters
PRC	People's Republic of China
PS	Preventive Service
PTO	Principal Trade Officer
ROC	Republic of China

SAS	Scandinavian Airlines Systems
STA	Short-Term Arrangement Regarding International Trade in Cotton Textiles
STO	Senior Trade Officer
TEXTAB	Textiles Advisory Board
TO	Trade Officer
TOGA	Trade Officer Grade Association
TSB	Textiles Surveillance Body (of the GATT, q.v., Textiles Committee)
UK	United Kingdom
UNCTAD	United Nations Conference on Trade and Development
UNDP	United Nations Development Programme
US	United States
USA	United States of America
WTO	World Trade Organisation, established in 1995 following the Uruguay round of trade negotiations. Not to be confused with the still-born ITO, q.v. See also Chapter Two
YESSS	Year-End Special Shipment Scheme

Note: References to 'dollars' in the text are to Hong Kong dollars unless otherwise specified.

Prologue

For one hundred and seventy years, Hong Kong has had to rely on its commitment to free trade and open markets for its survival. It has had to accept and adapt to the circumstances in which it found itself at any particular time. They have been such as to move the territory in incremental stages from entrepôt for China from the early 1840s to the 1940s, to entrepôt and manufacturing base from the late 1940s to the mid-1980s and, finally, from the mid-1980s to the present day, to entrepôt, manufacturing base, and service and financial centre.

My story covers Hong Kong's emergence as a major manufacturing base and the world's largest exporter of garments. This part of Hong Kong's history gave rise to an interesting paradox: Hong Kong had to limit its exports to preserve its trade. It had to subject its largest industry and employer of labour to a massive network of restrictions. Yet the more the restrictions tightened, the more prosperous Hong Kong became.

Protecting Free Trade tells the story of that paradox.

My book differs from others that cover this period in a number of ways. First, it is an unashamed encomium for a resilient population of several million people of variegated provenance. When I arrived in Hong Kong in 1958, they had no common spoken language, were crowded in a small territory of 1,000 square kilometres spread over 237 islands with no natural resources, and found themselves exposed, as Hong Kong began to achieve success, to the opprobrium of a number of countries, not least the metropolitan power whose dependent territory it supposedly was. Secondly, the book is a personal reminiscence of the thirty-odd years during which I had the privilege and pleasure of living and working in Hong Kong. It tells the story as seen by someone who was on the inside. As a civil servant in the Commerce and Industry Department for twenty years, I was directly involved in the trade and industry issues that affected Hong Kong. As chief executive of a Cantonese knitwear factory making ladies' sweaters in Hong Kong, China and Sri Lanka in the early 1980s, I became gamekeeper turned poacher (or *vice versa* depending on your point of view). As Director General of the Federation of Hong Kong Industries for four years, my task was to represent the interests of Hong Kong's manufacturing industries at a time when factories were beginning to relocate offshore and across the border, and Hong Kong began to move into the next phase of its development. Thirdly, my book does not seek to explain the paradox that arose in terms of economics. Rather it tells the story of the issues that confronted Hong Kong as the paradox developed, and the way in which the territory dealt with them, often with minimal support from the United Kingdom, frequently where its interests were directly opposite to those of Great Britain, and always as the underdog. Finally, I seek to convince the reader that five pieces of paper and the way Hong Kong put them to good use, played a significant role in its development. For, as I hope to show, they provided a strong defence of Hong Kong's interests in the many skirmishes the territory had with others over matters of trade. Many countries loudly praised Hong Kong's self-reliance and its determination to succeed. Still, they grumbled even more loudly about the 'floods of Hong Kong imports' as they called them, the only means the territory had of achieving its success. They were constantly seeking to limit the amounts they received. In reply, Hong Kong kept pointing to whichever of the five pieces of paper was relevant.

The move from entrepôt to manufacturing centre was at first overseen by an inexperienced and out-dated colonial government, a government that had to learn, step by step, how to react to a sequence of events totally beyond its ability to control. In the process, it was dragged reluctantly but inexorably into the effective and efficient governing *of* the people *for* the people. Until 1997, government *by* the people remained constitutionally located some six thousand miles away in the United Kingdom. Even so, it left Hong Kong very much to its own devices. Rather than turning to the metropolitan power, or international monetary funds or agencies of the United Nations for succour, Hong Kong found its salvation in the resilience of its people and its commitment to free trade and open markets. Government policies had to be made on the hoof to deal with situations that its civil servants had never experienced before, their only qualification for the task being a shared determination with those they governed to make the best of a very uncertain future.

Despite the many deficiencies of the book, what a great story there is to tell, and how exciting it was to be a very small part of it.

Part One

Five Pieces of Paper

Chapter One
Early Problems

The Second World War ended in 1945. Its aftermath marked a time of upheaval and change for victor and vanquished alike. For Great Britain, it meant the end of empire as nations, colonies, protectorates, trucial states and other sundry places under its administration gained their independence. Among the United Kingdom's few remaining dependent territories was Hong Kong. Although Britain was steadily dismantling its empire and returning sovereignty to the peoples of their native lands around the world, it stoutly refused to hand its Far Eastern outpost over to Generalissimo Chiang Kai-shek of the Kuomintang. Nor could it grant Hong Kong independence. To begin with, it had leased 90 percent of Hong Kong from China, so it was not actually Britain's to give away. A far more persuasive reason was that China would never have allowed it. Whenever the occasion offered, her statesmen drew attention to China's 'unequal treaties' with other countries. Everyone knew of whom they spoke. As Mr. Chou En-lai, China's Foreign Minister, so succinctly put it: Hong Kong, all of it, would revert to China 'when the time was ripe'. The late 1940s clearly did not represent such a time. So, Hong Kong had no choice in the matter.

For Hong Kong, the years immediately following the Second World War represented something of a swashbuckling era with survival the immediate priority. It was a British colony that had to get back on its feet following the Japanese occupation and also to deal with a growing number of refugees from the upheaval in China just across the Shum Chun River.

When Mao Tse-tung began his liberation of China, and Generalissimo Chiang Kai-shek took his government and, reportedly, a considerable amount of gold to Taiwan, Britain quickly recognised the new Chinese government. It then proceeded to ignore, equally quickly, the several hundred thousand Chinese who, not sharing Britain's enthusiasm for Chairman Mao's new regime, took up residence in its tiny colony. Shanty towns built of wooden packing cases and cardboard boxes soon covered the hillsides of Hong Kong Island and Kowloon. They were founded on nothing more than the conviction that these fragile habitations were to be preferred to the eventual prosperity Chairman Mao promised. The efforts of the Chairman's supporters to deny people access to the capitalist distractions of Hong Kong were more than matched by those who begged to differ. By 1952, over a million were estimated to have voted with their feet for Cardboard in preference to Communism. Christmas 1953 proved a turning point and the date from which Hong Kong's modern history might be said to begin. A massive fire swept through the shanty town at Shek Kip Mei. It finally forced the Hong Kong government to recognise that it had what the Colonial Secretary, Claude Burgess, described as a 'problem of people'. The government took two far-reaching decisions: first, to house the homeless and, second, to find them jobs. It was in the light of such unpromising beginnings that Hong Kong, comprising the island seized in 1841, a small part of the Kowloon peninsula, and a ninety-nine-year lease on the New Territories, set out to make its fortune, overseen by an inexperienced and outdated colonial government.

When I joined in 1958, as an Executive Officer, Class II, number sixty-seven on (and the bottom of) the seniority list, the government structure differed little from pre-war days. The top brass included the Governor, the Colonial Secretary, the Financial Secretary, the Secretary for Chinese Affairs (a Brit, of course) and the Heads of Departments. Administrative Officers, known as cadets and virtually all Brits, filled the top posts in the Colonial Secretariat and the departments. The middle management level consisted of the Executive Officers, mostly expats. Then came the Clerical Officers, all Chinese, who actually did the work. Alongside these 'generalists' stood the professionals — policemen, firemen, engineers and architects, among others, where the distinction between locals and expats appeared less pronounced. The arrival of expats from other British colonies often swelled the ranks of the 'professionals'. They had transferred to Hong Kong as their original places of work achieved independence.

Daily life was rather different from today as well. There were three sedan chairs at the bottom of Ice House Street which could be hired to carry you up the slope to mid-levels for some exorbitant fare — about two dollars, as I recall, with others at Taikoo Sugar Refinery at North Point.

The 'new' Star Ferry terminal remained the subject of grumbles because of the distance one had to walk to board; previously the ferries had come alongside and you just hopped on. They charged you five cents for second class and ten cents if you wanted to travel on the upper deck. At the Hong Kong Island terminal, a long line of Mercedes-Benz taxis waited for customers; flag fall one dollar fifty cents while on the Kowloon side, just one dollar. Also at the Star Ferry, numerous rickshaws competed for business at fifty cents for so many minutes.

My wife and I lived in a three-bedroom apartment on the fifth floor of a 'private tenancy' in MacDonnell Road (because of the dearth of government quarters) with a nice view of Government House and the harbour beyond. The rent was HK$950 a month of which I paid $50 and the government the rest. I could afford to run a second-hand Austin A40. Its registration number plate, HK520, probably would command a fortune now if it still existed. We hired a live-in *amah*, could afford the monthly subs of the cricket and football clubs, maintained a credit of two hundred dollars with Shui Tai, our *comprador*, and ate out at Jimmy's Kitchen or Maxim's or the Paramount Restaurant once a fortnight. I always took lunch at the China Fleet Club just opposite Police Headquarters in Arsenal Street: breaded prawns, chips, a glass of San Mig and a game of snooker.

I obtained my car driving licence in 1959. You could do it in one of three ways. For Chinese, they paid a considerable sum of money to an expatriate police sub-inspector (local officers being suspected of too much leniency) who then placed the sought after 'PASS' chop on the application form. For expatriates who knew someone in the police, they spent a pleasant half an hour chatting in the front seat of the car and then received the necessary chop. For the rest, they actually took the test, hoping for the best. At the time I took the test, I was working in Police Headquarters and had considerable difficulty in persuading anybody that I really wanted things done properly. I remember that traffic volumes were such that I was able to do my three-point turn and emergency stop outside the Helena May on Garden Road.

Road space was shared by a few private cars, mostly British made, buses, trams, taxis, rickshaws and tricycles. The latter had a large red box container at the front, and provided an effective and efficient goods delivery service around town. Immaculately uniformed police constables with pristine white gauntlets regulated the whole, choreographing the movements of traffic at busy junctions with balletic arm and hand gestures from pagoda-roofed pedestals.

In summer, we packed winter clothing away in camphor-wood chests to protect them from the heat and humidity, and placed them in Dairy Farm's cold storage. Lane Crawford (up-market) and Whiteaways (mid-market) provided goods from 'home', while China Products sold everything at unbelievably low prices. Every expat family used a *comprador* to deliver anything you wanted twice a day and extend a month's credit before asking for payment. Every Christmas, he would deliver a bottle of wine or a turkey as a present which regulations specifically excluded from the definition of 'corrupt gifts' under the law. You hired at least one Chinese *amah*. She expected (and received) a thirteen-month salary every year, the thirteenth payable at Chinese New Year, when deafening fire-crackers celebrated the departure of one animal from the Chinese zodiac and the arrival of the next.

Looking back, sixty years later, these seemed to have been halcyon days for the expat. The local may not wax quite so nostalgic. Such days were not to last much longer.

For Hong Kong stood out as a rather irritating pimple of entrepreneurial activity on the bottom of the map of the world's largest socialist country. As the years passed, it became the target of hypocritical hyperbole from developed countries who claimed to sympathise with Hong Kong's delicate situation and applauded its efforts to achieve self-reliance, but then loudly complained about the 'floods of imports' by which it sought to do so. Nor did Hong Kong have many friends among the developing countries who became increasingly jealous of the territory's growing success. Perhaps, remaining the last significant jewel in the British imperial crown became Hong Kong's greatest sin. Where others had thrown off the shackles of colonialism and were in a right old mess, Hong Kong continued to move steadily from strength to strength, something colonies supposedly did not do. By the late 1970s, Hong Kong had become the world's largest exporter of clothing, and the thirteenth largest exporter (of some 135) in the world overall. As unofficial leader of the developing countries in matters affecting textiles and clothing, it was seen as a tough but reasonable negotiator and respected for its efforts to live up to its beliefs and international obligations. It was voted year after year as the best place in the world in which to do business (and still is).

It achieved all these without a cent of financial help from anyone. As Hong Kong's man in London, Earnest Grimwood, was wont to put it 'The colony not only had to pull itself up by its own bootstraps, it had to make the bloody things in the first place.' The hundreds of thousands who, preferring capitalism to communism, crossed into Hong Kong from China in the early fifties, had brought with them a wide range of skills as well as a pressing need to find outlets for their expertise. A happy compromise emerged as to how this might be accomplished: the market would decide how the skills were to be used, while the government would seek to create a stable environment in which business could flourish under the rule of law. This was no formal solution agreed upon following consultation between governing and governed: it just happened that way. The *laissez-faire* approach undoubtedly derived from Hong Kong's historical role as a free port, with no point in it being anything else. From the beginning, Hong Kong had served as an entrepôt for China. By the time Chairman Mao had come to power, it had already developed into China's busiest port. Although not much went into China, whatever trade there was usually went through Hong Kong. There was however plenty of goods coming from China, earning much needed foreign currency for the People's Republic, and providing Hong Kong with welcome economic side benefits.

In addition to its port, Hong Kong possessed a small industrial base, mainly Cantonese-owned factories, producing such goods as preserved ginger, a motley array of towels, embroidered table cloths and place mats and enamelware, exported largely to West Africa. There were none of the protective import duties then common in other countries because there was nothing to protect and emerging industries needed access to raw materials from the cheapest sources worldwide. The new residents from China included entrepreneurs from Shanghai who had owned spinning and weaving mills there. They reestablished their operations in Hong Kong, providing not only industrial diversification but a challenge to the local and somewhat old-fashioned Cantonese textile industry. Business began to pick up, creating jobs while the Colony's output started to grow. By the late 1950s, Hong Kong exported most of its production, mainly to other South East Asian countries and some to the United Kingdom, although how much and to whom, remained unclear.

The collection of trade data was the responsibility of the Statistics Branch of the Commerce and Industry Department. However, it was not until 1960 that Hong Kong finally separated domestic exports from re-exports. Domestic exports consist of goods produced in Hong Kong while re-exports represent goods imported into Hong Kong, then shipped out again to other destinations without undergoing any processing. By the mid-1950s, the inability to distinguish between domestic and re-exports was giving rise to increasing suspicion that some of Hong Kong's exports were in fact made elsewhere, and passed off as Hong Kong products. In particular, Japan had been a major supplier of cheap goods to Europe before the war. Afterwards, its trade became subject to many restrictions. A nearby free port such as Hong Kong might clearly tempt enterprising traders to use the port to export prohibited Japanese goods into its former markets in Europe and America. China trade posed yet another problem. While Chairman Mao had added the word 'People's' to the country's title to create the People's Republic of China (PRC), the Generalissimo had taken what remained of his Republic of China (ROC) to Taiwan, which he pretended was China proper. The United States of America, who could not bear the thought of a billion 'Red China commies' opposite them just across the Pacific, shared this pretence. In 1950, the USA introduced legislation under its Foreign Assets Control Regulations that banned all imports from the People's Republic of China. Further, it also prohibited the import of any goods from any country that had used raw materials from the PRC. It added North Korea as well for good measure. It was obvious that a smart trader in Hong Kong might try to circumvent FAC Regulations by importing Chinese goods into Hong Kong, changing the origin labels on the products and exporting them to the USA. The potential competition between true Hong Kong products and those made elsewhere and subsequently relabelled in Hong Kong clearly undermined its efforts to establish a domestic manufacturing industry. It also threatened Hong Kong's international reputation. The absence of separate export statistics muddied the waters still further while, perhaps, providing a convenient cover for those who did not want trade activity too closely scrutinised.

Thus, no sooner had Hong Kong begun to deal with its 'problem of people' than a 'problem of products' began to emerge. The problem with products was two-fold. Although the population had more than doubled, clearly, the total Hong Kong market remained too small to sustain the volume of goods its nascent industries now produced. South East Asia offered a wider market of sorts albeit small, while many countries in the region maintained import restrictions on the types of products Hong Kong was making. Thus, an urgent need existed to find bigger and better markets abroad, in Europe and the USA, for example, in order for the government to achieve its goal of creating full employment. The other issue involved securing access to those larger markets and persuading them that a Hong Kong product indeed represented what it claimed. Much of this occurred before I arrived but I was aware of some of the issues as I had been working in an import house in London before coming to Hong Kong.

On my arrival, I was asked whether I had given any thought to the department I would like to join. Someone had tipped me off that the Commerce and

Industry Department[1] offered a good posting. There was a lot happening there, he had said, and the chance to travel. So, I explained to the Establishment Officer that I had been working in an import house in London for three years doing business with Hong Kong and suggested that the DC&I might put my knowledge and skills to good use. The next day, they posted me to the civilian staff of the Hong Kong Police Force. After a year in PHQ and the pulling of appropriate strings, I was posted in November 1959 to the Commerce and Industry Department and stayed there for the next twenty-odd years.

The 1959 organisation chart of the department throws interesting light on how the government perceived Hong Kong's trade priorities, as well as on its management structure. The Director of Commerce and Industry, H. A. 'Ginger' Angus, who reported directly to the Financial Secretary, headed it. A Deputy Director, Dermont Barty, who had transferred from the Indian Civil Service after Independence, supported him. He dealt with 'general administration' and 'statistics'. Two Assistant Directors, George Hole and Pat Dodge, oversaw 'Controls' and 'Preventive Service' and 'Trade Promotion', 'Industry' and 'Certification of Origin' respectively. A young Administrative Officer, David Akers-Jones, handled 'Trade Licensing', 'Dutiable Commodities' and 'Supplies'. These gentlemen formed the 'Directorate', which included Akers-Jones, due to his status as an Administrative Officer although he did not hold a directorate position. The organisational hierarchy comprised Directorate, Branch and Section. The department consisted of eight branches. The first, the Preventive Service (PS), the uniformed precursor of the present Customs and Excise Department, was charged with anti-smuggling duties and protecting the public revenue arising from the five commodities that attracted excise taxes. It also undertook factory inspections and consignment checks. The second, the Supplies Branch, ensured that the colony maintained a three-month supply of rice, corned beef, coal and firewood. The third, the Dutiable Commodities Branch, headed by an Assistant Trade Officer (ATO), collected the revenue

---

[1]   The Commerce and Industry Department was the official name of the department at this time. Customers in trade and industry always knew it as the Department of Commerce and Industry, or DC&I, for short. It could not use the abbreviation CID to avoid confusion with the Police. I use the form DC&I hereafter for convenience. Later, it became a 'federal' department comprising three separate but interrelated departments — Trade Department, Industry Department and the Customs and Excise Department, headed by the Director of Trade, Industry and Customs, known as D-TIC. Later still, after I had left Hong Kong, the name and structure changed again.

arising from excise duties on ethyl alcohol (wines, spirits and beer, among others, and some perfumes), the elegantly named table waters, hydrocarbon oils (i.e. petrol), tobacco and methyl alcohol. The fourth, the Statistics Branch, headed by Cyril Stratton, faced the unenviable task of trying to keep track of the arrival and departure of goods, into and from Hong Kong, their points of origin and their destinations. The fifth, the Trade Licensing Branch also headed by an ATO, handled import and export licensing. The sixth, the Industry and Certification Branch, contained sections dealing with 'Industry' (headed by Jimmy McGregor, Acting Trade Officer); 'Certification' (led by Alan Trickett, also Acting Trade Officer) along with sections that gathered industry statistics (Acting Trade Officer, Len Dunning) and issued various types of certification (Executive Officers, Class II) and 'Industry Inspections'. The seventh, the Export Promotion Branch, supervised by a Senior Trade Officer (STO), assisted by Bill Dorward, Acting Trade Officer, comprised two sections (headed by ATOs) — 'Trade Publications and Library (one bookcase!) Section' and 'Trade Enquiries, Trade Fairs, Business Visitors, etc. Section' [*sic*]. Listed among the staff in this section is one L. W. R. Mills, Executive Officer. Finally, the eighth, the Overseas Trade Relations Branch, comprised one STO. No one quite understood its function. The STO, beavered away in a small office on the fourth floor of the Fire Brigade Building, and communicated upwards with the Directorate from time to time but rarely with the hoi polloi below. Some ten years later, this one-man show had transmogrified into the Commercial Relations Divisions of DC&I and, subsequently, became the Trade Department.

The Administration and Finance Branch kept meticulous records of how late we were for the office, how much leave each of us was due or had taken, how much money we had spent, whether we had receipts (no receipt, no reimbursement), and made sure that we all travelled using the right class of transport and stayed at hotels with the correct number of stars when we were overseas. This nonsense came to an abrupt halt when I was appointed secretary to a Hong Kong Trade Mission to Australia in 1961. The mission was led by 'Duggie' Clague (later Sir Douglas Clague). Under the rules, Unofficials were entitled to first class travel and five-star hotels. Civil servants were accommodated and travelled at the level appropriate to their ranking in the hierarchy. Thus, when we travelled to Australia, the other five members of our group, including Dermont Barty, Deputy Director of Commerce and Industry, flew first class and stayed at top hotels throughout. I had to fly economy class, which required me to leave the plane first so that I could run around to the front of the plane to join the other members and meet the welcoming party. The hotel situation was even more ridiculous. As I was only a junior, I had to stay in a different hotel altogether. And being too junior to qualify for taxi travel, I had to catch a bus to the hotel where the others were staying to rejoin the party. Duggie Clague declared 'enough', and insisted I travel and stay with the rest of them. The hapless Dermont Barty spent the rest of the trip worrying about how he would explain this to the Director when we returned to Hong Kong. The rules were eventually changed. The Export Promotion Branch kept me very busy. Trade was growing, and the significance of the first piece of paper to which this story relates rapidly became apparent as importing countries sought ways to limit the flow of goods from Hong Kong.

Chapter Two
The GATT: The First Piece of Paper

Acronyms abound in the world of trade, but probably none holds greater importance than the GATT, the General Agreement on Tariffs and Trade.

The GATT has been around since 1947. It continues as the internationally accepted instrument governing world trade, and is now the responsibility of the World Trade Organisation, established in 1995. Earlier, towards the close of the Second World War, the soon-to-be victorious allies sought to establish ways and means of co-operating in order to move as smoothly and as swiftly as possible from a war footing to normalcy once the fighting had ceased. The United Nations Monetary and Financial Conference, better known as the Bretton Woods Conference, for its venue in New Hampshire, USA, constituted one of the most important conferences to this end. Some forty-four nations attended in 1944. Its core consideration was the idea that world trade markets should be open to all. Previously, individual countries had pursued narrow national interests through bilateral or plurilateral treaties among themselves. While it was tacitly acknowledged that national interest, as the country concerned defined it, would always take precedence, there was a genuine desire to put an end to trade blocks and spheres of influence. This could be achieved, it was argued, if the major democratic industrial countries lowered barriers to trade and freed up the movement of capital. In furtherance of these ideals, they agreed that they should establish an International Trade Organisation (ITO) to administer the rules set down for the governance of international trade. Everything proceeded apace — they drew up an ITO charter, and agreed it at the United Nations Conference on Trade and Employment held in Havana, Cuba in 1948. Then the roof fell in. The United States Senate, which has authority in such matters, refused to ratify the charter. In the Senate's view, the US could not agree to any treaty that exercised or implied supremacy over the government of the United States of America. As a result, the ITO never saw the light of day. All was not lost however. Concurrently, a group of nations continued to work in Geneva on a set of rules to govern international trade that it had intended the ITO should administer. They presented a draft 'General Agreement on Tariffs and Trade' (the GATT), an instrument designed to encourage freer trade among member states (known as Contracting Parties) by regulating and reducing tariffs on traded goods and by providing a common mechanism for resolving trade disputes. However, since the GATT rules also implied supremacy over those who subscribed to them, again, the USA refused to accept it.

Civil servants revel in devising solutions to such problems. They soon found a means not only to give effect to the GATT but to do so in a way that would commit all parties to follow its provisions without having formally to accept it. The solution is to be found in the words of the Protocol of Provisional Application of the GATT which stated that the countries signing it undertook '... to apply [its Articles] provisionally on and after I January 1948 ...'. In other words, they would all accept the rules as laid down but only provisionally and not formally. Even the USA could sign up for that.[1] The original eight signatories to the Protocol of Provisional Application were Australia, Belgium, Canada, France, Luxembourg, the Netherlands, the United Kingdom of Great Britain and Northern Ireland, and the United States of America. The Preamble to the GATT lists those countries who were 'desirous of contributing to [the] objectives [of the GATT] by entering into reciprocal and mutually advantageous arrangements' to reduce tariffs and other barriers to trade substantially and to eliminate discriminatory treatment in international commerce. The countries named were Australia, Belgium, Brazil, Canada, Ceylon [*sic*], Chile, the Republic of China (i.e. before Chairman Mao's liberation), Cuba, Czechoslovakia, France, India, Lebanon, Luxembourg, the Netherlands, New Zealand, Norway, Pakistan, Southern Rhodesia [*sic*], Syria, South Africa, the United Kingdom of Great Britain and Northern Ireland, and the United States of America. Thus no country ever formally ratified the most important

---

[1]   The Uruguay Round of international trade negotiations resuscitated the idea of an international trade organisation. In 1995, forty-seven years after the ITO had fallen over, the USA changed its mind and the signatories established the World Trade Organisation (WTO) to govern international trade. By this time, the emergence and increasing cohesion of the European Union counterbalanced the original overweening economic power of the USA. The WTO now holds the responsibility for the implementation, operation and upholding of the '1947 GATT', which, with its elaborations and notes, comprises the book of rules that currently governs the conduct of international trade.

instrument ever to govern world trade or accepted it as legally binding. Yet, all member countries followed it more or less to the letter for the next forty-seven years until the founding of the WTO in 1995.

Article I, paragraph 1, of the GATT is headed 'General Most-Favoured-Nation Treatment'.

Its somewhat convoluted text essentially states that one country cannot discriminate against another in any area having to do with trade. It is phrased rather less starkly than that: every member country that is a member of the GATT must afford every other member the same treatment in matters of trade as that member offers its 'most-favoured' trading partner. The Article establishes what has become known in trade parlance as 'the most-favoured nation principle of non-discrimination' or simply 'the MFN principle'.

Back in 1947, few would have given any thought to the possibility that the provisional application of the GATT would have particular significance as regards a small, inconsequential British colony tucked away on the coast of southern China — least of all Hong Kong itself. The absence of any reference to the GATT in the DC&I organisation chart for 1959 suggests the department did not fully appreciate its crucial significance for Hong Kong. The GATT holds such importance for Hong Kong primarily because it places all GATT members on an equal footing and forbids discriminatory trade practices. As far as trade was concerned, miniscule Hong Kong and the giant USA and the even larger European Community[2] in later years were each bound by the same rules, and faced each other as equals across the negotiating table. Even if in the

---

[2] The European Community has been known by a number of names (not all of them polite). It began as the European Economic Community in 1955, widely known as the EEC or the 'Common Market' or 'the Six' (the original member countries). When others joined, it became the European Community or 'the EC' or just 'the Community' (as people refer to 'the States' to mean the USA). It was also called 'the Nine' when the UK, Ireland and Denmark joined, and 'the Twelve' with the accession of Spain, Portugal and Greece. When those countries who had established the European Free Trade Association (EFTA) as a counterweight to the EEC either defected and joined the EEC or were accepted as part of the European Community without the commitments of full membership of the Community, the group became known as the European Union, the term used today.

Rather than using the correct title and applying it to the group at any one period covered by the book, I have used the terms 'EEC and 'Community' interchangeably throughout to mean whichever group name applied at the time in the hope this will make for easier reading and avoid confusion.

real world, Goliath rather than David tends to win, the GATT served to impose some limits on what one country might do to another it did not particularly like, had the GATT not existed. No developed country wanted to be seen publicly bashing the poorer countries and especially the few that, like Hong Kong, were making a real effort to rely on hard work rather than hand-outs for their future well-being. Nor, in the wider world, did they want to be seen ignoring the ground rules. Others, more powerful in economic and political terms than Hong Kong, might want to treat them in the same way.

The GATT is nothing if not flexible. Article I, paragraph 2(a) states that the provisions of Article I, paragraph 1 (the MFN paragraph) do not require the elimination of any preferences in respect of import duties or charges in force exclusively between two or more of the territories listed in GATT Annex A. Annex A lists, along with some other countries, the 'United Kingdom of Great Britain and Northern Ireland' and 'Dependent territories of the United Kingdom of Great Britain and Northern Ireland ...' of which Hong Kong was, of course, one. This meant that the trade preferences that existed between the UK and Hong Kong overrode the MFN rule of Article I, paragraph 1, which would otherwise have required the UK to offer the same preferences to all other countries not listed in Annex A but members of the GATT. The parties allowed this apparent conflict to stand and justified it on the shaky grounds that it represented a pre-existing trade arrangement and possibly, since, at the time, Britain had rather more influence, or perhaps sympathisers, than it does today. Further, of course, a number of significant British Commonwealth trading nations thought they stood to benefit from such preferences.[3] GATT Article XXVI, paragraph 5(a) declares that each government accepting the Agreement does so in respect of its metropolitan territory and of 'the other territories for which it has international responsibility'. This meant that the UK accepted the GATT on behalf of Hong Kong, among others. Of course, it did not mention Hong Kong by name, which was nowhere to be seen at this stage.

Bringing all these threads together in the context of Hong Kong's interests in the late 1940s and early 1950s, three facts emerge. Firstly, Hong Kong became a member of the GATT by virtue of the United Kingdom accepting the GATT on behalf of its dependent territories. Secondly, member countries of the GATT,

---

[3]   In fact, preferential agreements act in restraint of trade: they exclude the unpreferred while intra-preference area trading discourages access to cheaper raw materials outside the area because of higher import duties into the preference area.

with whom Hong Kong traded, could not discriminate against Hong Kong's exports and had to offer Hong Kong the same terms as they offered their most-favoured trading partner. On the other side of the coin, Hong Kong had to treat imports from GATT members on an equal basis. This presented no problems for Hong Kong since it operated a completely free port, open to all. It also meant that Hong Kong manufacturers could buy their raw materials in the cheapest market wherever that might be. It did not stipulate that Hong Kong had to buy from British Commonwealth sources. Indeed, such a requirement would have been in conflict with the MFN principle. Thirdly, as a member of GATT but also having a preferential arrangement on tariffs with the United Kingdom, Hong Kong had access, as of right, to the UK market under the GATT together with a significant duty advantage over other GATT Contracting Parties, not members of the Commonwealth Preference Area.

Hong Kong's entitlement to such preferences stemmed from a 1932 conference held in Ottawa in which the dominions (Australia, Canada, New Zealand, Newfoundland and South Africa) and the British colonies participated to discuss ways and means of avoiding a recurrence of the Great Depression. It resulted in the Ottawa Agreements, which established the concept of Imperial Preference. They provided for low or nil tariffs on trade among the countries and territories that made up the then British Empire, and high tariffs on imports from non-Empire countries. The objective was to expand intra-Empire trade. The signatories seemed to have overlooked the fact that since high tariffs reduced the incentive for those outside the preference area to export to those within it, the Commonwealth countries were, first, limiting their choice of needed imports, for example raw materials, and, second, acting in restraint of trade rather that expanding it: see footnote 3 above. Thus, when economic and social imperatives required Hong Kong to look beyond South East Asia for markets for its products, it held an advantageous position. It had right of access to the United Kingdom and could obtain preferential entry for its goods as well, plus equal standing with other exporting countries when shipping to Europe or the United States. At this stage, Hong Kong was very much in a win-win-win situation.

With the GATT having established Hong Kong's right of access for its goods to overseas markets, the next problem became to persuade those countries to which Hong Kong had access rights, that a Hong Kong product indeed represented what it purported to be. In order to achieve this, the roles of a number of key Hong Kong players — traders, manufacturers and government — had, of necessity, to change significantly. As the 1950s progressed, local entrepreneurs took increasing advantage of Hong Kong's membership of the GATT and the trading opportunities presented by Imperial Preference. The import company I was working for in London was inundated with new samples from old and new suppliers. The long-established *hongs* (large companies) in Hong Kong, most of them British-owned, had traditionally dominated importing and exporting. They saw the business advantages inherent in the growing demand for imported raw materials and in exporting beyond South East Asia to the larger and more lucrative markets of Europe, the USA and, especially, the United Kingdom. Manufacturers, for their part, possessed little knowledge of their overseas customers or the way to reach them. All the time the orders came in, manufacturers were happy to leave such matters to the exporters, some of whom deliberately withheld customer information from manufacturers to protect their own business. The benefit for the manufacturers was that they had not to worry about such things as fashion trends and design; the exporters told them what customers wanted, and showed manufacturers something to copy, who then produced the goods. The exporters took responsibility for delivery to the end customer. But a few Chinese companies began to enter into the export trade and one or two of the largest manufacturers, mostly in spinning and weaving, set up their own export departments.

On the industry side, the government facilitated the establishment of the Federation of Hong Kong Industries in 1960 to counterbalance the Chinese Manufacturers Association, a truly independent group, sometimes too effective, that is to say outspoken, for the government's liking. The government believed so strongly that the Federation should represent the industry, that it gave them a small, temporary subsidy, something unheard of in *laissez-faire* Hong Kong. This temporary assistance finally disappeared when a rejuvenated Federation became self-sufficient some twenty-five years later. At about the same time, a working party was established to consider whether trade promotion should be hived off from the DC&I and responsibility for 'trade development', a somewhat nebulous phrase in terms of definition, passed to an independent Hong Kong Trade Development Council (HKTDC).

Imports from Hong Kong drew a growing number of complaints overseas about labour conditions and wages in Hong Kong factories as well as the quality, safety and price of Hong Kong products. The strong demand for Hong Kong goods clearly proved that these criticisms did not originate from consumers. Rather, they came from domestic suppliers who found their products displaced, applied pressure upon their governments to act and used safety, quality, and factory conditions, among others, as excuses for protection. To the extent it could, the Hong Kong government resisted these pressures. When, in 1958, the UK government approached Hong Kong regarding wages and factory conditions, the response was uncharacteristically robust. In carefully chosen words, the Governor, Sir Robert Black, pointed out that at that time standards, as the word was understood in the western world, had to go by the board. Hong Kong people and the government were more concerned with survival. Increased prosperity was a longer-term goal built upon and sustained by a sound economy. Current Hong Kong government policies were influenced much more by what could be done rather than what should be done. The government's immediate concern was to get and keep as many people in work as possible, not introduce labour legislation whose effect could be to worsen conditions for all. On the subject of quality, the government made it clear this was a matter that the marketplace would resolve. Under UK law, manufacturers could mark products from Hong Kong either 'Made in Hong Kong' or 'Empire Made'. Wary importers were worried that full identification of a Hong Kong product's origin might arouse protectionist sentiment or affect sales. They plumped for 'Empire Made'. Since no other supplier used this mark however, it became synonymous with Hong Kong and, worse, with doubtful quality, uncertain durability and low price. Some products merited the criticism. On the other hand, items such as yarns, piece-goods and some garments and electronic products were of good quality and competitively priced. The Hong Kong government also came under pressure to certify prices quoted in invoices in order to eliminate under-invoicing as a way in which a company could reduce import duties. The government refused point-blank to enter into any discussion on price with other governments or overseas companies. Again, it argued that price reflected market forces and had nothing to do with the government. DC&I was even asked to certify that exports to Arab countries had no Israeli content. Again, the government refused to act. Since at least one Hong Kong manufacturer was successfully exporting tin hats to Egypt for its 1967 war with Israel without problems, this seemed a political rather than an economic issue. The Hong Kong government faced more than enough Far Eastern problems without involving itself in Middle Eastern affairs as well.

Despite the public stance the government took on factory conditions, price, and quality, it was rather more concerned with these issues in private than it appeared to be in public. All of them were providing ammunition for those intent on bashing Hong Kong. So, when I was transferred to the Commerce and Industry Department, I headed the newly-established Trade Complaints Section. It became the repository of all letters grumbling about Hong Kong products and provided a useful insight into the state of our industry, what it manufactured and what was happening in the real world of business. We were charged with dealing with these complaints but without any authority to do so. Upon receipt of a complaint, the Section would attempt to track down the manufacturer, and use its good offices, that is to say, to point out how awkward life might become for a company who upset the DC&I and to persuade the errant producer to replace the product or refund the price the consumer had paid. Where we succeeded, we would send a conciliatory letter to the complainant assuring him or her that the mistake on the part of the manufacturer was an aberration. It would seek to reassure that the vast majority of Hong Kong products were of the highest quality 'commensurate with price' which was always the tag line of such letters. They concluded on the hopeful note that a replacement product or a British postal order for 17/6d or some such amount would follow shortly, with the comforting assertion that the writer remained the recipient's obedient servant.

Some of the letters of complaint served to lighten our task. Many, especially from the USA, arrived addressed to 'Hong Kong, Japan'. Others of similar provenance, but clearly from more informed consumers, were addressed to 'B.C.C. Hong Kong, Red China', that is, the British Crown Colony of Hong Kong, whether in ignorance of their own country's position on colonies or in the hope of spiting Chairman Mao is not known. The Brits probably were the most vociferous in their letters, but also more entertaining.

Unbeknownst to higher authority, we kept a collection of the best for several years, until the HKTDC assumed responsibility for dealing with trade complaints.

One such complaint letter began: 'When my son put his Nelsom [*sic*] telescope to his eye, it fell out'. Another reported, 'I took advantage of a trip to Hong Kong to visit the factory. The first thing to strike me was the workers'. Another stated that, 'The flashing lamp came as something of a shock'. Finally, one writer claimed, 'When I picked up the tin car I bought for my son, it gave me a small prick'. There was broad consensus that even DC&I could do little to help in such a situation and that a 17/6d postal order would offer little consolation.

At this point, I decided on a career change. The Export Promotion Branch had created an additional ATO post and I succeeded in transferring from Executive Officer, Class II to Assistant Trade Officer. It marked my second attempt; I had tried once before when working in Police Headquarters. It represented a significant step up the ladder for the ATO drew the same salary as an Executive Officer, Class I, a rank I harboured no expectation of reaching within three years of joining the government.

I was immediately thrown into Hong Kong's tentative efforts to promote exports. The DC&I took part in trade fairs in such exotic places as Sydney and San Francisco and I participated as a member of the Hong Kong delegation to the Lagos International Trade Fair, an experience the telling of which would fill another book. Later, as I have mentioned, I was appointed Secretary to a public/private sector trade mission to Australia. We established a Trade Enquiries Service. Anyone asking for names and addresses of manufacturers of a particular product could expect a speedy but less than helpful response. Higher authorities decreed that a government department should not distribute selective lists. So, if five hundred factories made T-shirts or enamel spittoons, the department would forward all five hundred names to the enquirer, each one produced on an ageing stencil machine that printed the letters 'e' and 'o' as solid black blobs. We had to wait for the next financial year before we could purchase a new one. We launched the *Hong Kong Trade Bulletin*, a monthly magazine published by the DC&I. Intended to create awareness of, and arouse interest in, the increasing range of products that Hong Kong had to offer the world, its turgid prose and grainy black and white photographs must have dissuaded as many buyers as it enticed. But it represented a start. It even carried paid advertisements for exporters and manufacturers brave enough to be publicly identified as the source of much that was nasty, but had the redeeming feature for the consumer of the day of being cheap and desirable as recovery from a devastating world war got under way. The late 1950s were different times from now. A strict moral code applied to the *Bulletin*. The government thought lady models in its publications inappropriate so they were banned. One daring Trade Officer, Len Dunning, as I recall, later snapped up by the HKTDC and eventually its dynamic head, despairing of making Hong Kong beaded sweaters fixed to a board with drawing pins look alluring, arranged to photograph them on shapely models, then airbrushed away head, arms and other body parts to leave a shapely but disembodied product and quite a lot to the imagination. So it was with anything undignified or suggestive, however big the market. One of Hong Kong's best-selling lines to West Africa at the time was the brightly coloured enamel chamber pot daubed with stirring slogans calling for freedom for Africa. The government banned it from the publication as well as a novelty donkey that dispensed cork-tipped cigarettes from the end opposite to its head when its ear was pulled.

I was posted to the *Hong Kong Trade Bulletin* for a year. Jeff Ridge, a young Administrative Officer with a degree from Oxford in modern and Byzantine Greek, joined the department. Supposedly, he and I jointly edited the *Bulletin*. We became lifelong friends and found our duties both amusing and frustrating. Not only had we to exercise care not to affront public decency with our photos, but we had to pass every feature article up the organisational ladder to the Director himself to obtain approval before its publication. Our texts had retained little of their original flair and wit by the time we received them back as they passed through the hands of the Trade Officer, the Senior Trade Officer, the Assistant Director and the Director himself, each adding his own 'polish' to the drafts. On one occasion, I wrote an article on Hong Kong's plastic flowers, and, tongue firmly in cheek, borrowed a couple of lines for a title from Shakespeare's 'Antony and Cleopatra': 'Age cannot wither nor custom stale their infinite variety'. I was astonished to find this was the only bit remaining of the original draft with a comment in the margin 'Very good, Mills', from the Director. Until that moment, I had thought he did not know I even existed. Early editions of the *Trade Bulletin* gave little hint that one day, in the hands of the Hong Kong Trade Development Council, it would re-emerge as the HKTDC's *Enterprise*. It ultimately found its way into the *Guinness World Records* as the monthly magazine with the highest number of pages in the world, most of them ads with lots of pretty girls.

These were happy days, but in 1963, I was moved on as another issue which had been smouldering for some time flared up. I often thought it appropriate that we were housed in Fire Brigade Building. It involved a number of questions regarding the origin of products, a subject the government took very seriously indeed.

Chapter Three
The Certificate of Origin:
The Second Piece of Paper

It is probably fair to say that not too many people have stopped to consider the question as to what confers origin on a product. It sounds pretty dull stuff, and, these days, apart from mild surprise to find something not 'Made in China', people manage to get on with their lives unaffected by such matters.

In the immediate post-war years, however, origin was of considerable importance and for governments a matter of substantial concern. This was because import duties were used as a means to protect domestic industries or to grant preferential rates to those with special relationships with the importing country.

As a result of many rounds of trade negotiations over the years under the auspices of the GATT, import tariffs worldwide have reached an all-time low. For the most part, the origin of a product has now more to do with establishing membership of free trade areas and common markets[1] and with examining origin criteria to ensure they do not constitute a hidden restraint on trade. The use of the import duty as a means of protection has virtually disappeared.

In the 1950s, many countries maintained restrictions against Japan, as did several Western European countries to imports from Iron Curtain countries. The USA would have nothing to do with products from China (PRC) or North Korea. Despite and because of Article I of the GATT, several countries offered preferential terms to favoured nations and territories, while the

---

[1]   In a free trade area, the countries involved agree that trade among themselves of their own products should be free of duty, while their individual domestic customs tariffs apply to imports from others. In a common market, known as a 'customs union', goods, regardless of origin, move freely among the common market countries, once those from outside the union have paid a common external customs tariff upon import. The GATT sanctioned both regimes (Article XXIV). The Certificate of Origin helps to identify those goods not entitled to the benefits of the free trade area or customs union.

European Economic Community (the Common Market or EEC) emerged in 1956, and, later, the European Free Trade Area (EFTA). All of these, therefore, had an interest in the origin of the products they imported. Understandably, questions surfaced about Hong Kong products given its free port status, its proximity to China, North Korea and Japan, its right of access to all the major markets of the world under the GATT and its entitlement to Commonwealth Preference. Furthermore, because Hong Kong possessed no natural resources of its own, and necessarily imported all of its raw materials, countries wanted to know precisely which processes carried out in Hong Kong distinguished a domestic export from a re-export. They wanted to know also how they could verify it since Hong Kong trade statistics did not separate one from the other. By the end of the 1950s, it was estimated that Hong Kong shipped one-fifth of its total domestic exports to the United Kingdom and the remainder principally to West Germany (its name then), to the Benelux countries (Belgium, the Netherlands and Luxembourg) as well as to Scandinavia. Only France resisted the onslaught, steadfastly refusing to remove restrictions on imports from Hong Kong, contrary to the GATT. South East Asia and West Africa continued to offer reasonable markets. Across the Pacific Ocean, the USA was becoming a popular market for Hong Kong because of the large size of its orders and the resultant longer, more efficient production runs for Hong Kong factories. The variety of products continued to grow as well. Enamelware was slowly losing out to plastic household ware. Plastic flowers from Hong Kong virtually wiped out the Italian artificial flower industry. The new and revolutionary transistor radio was being assembled from imported components. Exports of preserved ginger to Australia were booming, and Japan could never get enough China Sea prawns. Hong Kong shipped yarns and grey cloth in quantity to the UK, and found a new market there for the tablecloths and place mats of the Cantonese textile industry. Garments grew the fastest of all items. Clearly, Hong Kong needed to give some assurances on origin quickly if building protectionist pressures were not to nip Hong Kong's growing trade in the bud. The reliance of many countries at that time on self-certification, that is, the manufacturer merely stated on the invoice that the goods originated in X country, and this assertion was accepted at face value, did not help matters.

The Hong Kong government decided that it had no choice but to enter the certification of origin business in a big way. It handed the task to the Commerce and Industry Department, and the second piece of paper — the Certificate of Hong Kong Origin — emerged to provide a solid foundation for Hong Kong's trade and industry. As a first step, it sought to establish what constituted Hong Kong origin — a task not as simple as it might sound, especially for a territory that imported all or most of the raw materials for the goods it manufactured. To take an extreme example, a lady's woollen sweater might include wool from New Zealand, spun into yarns and dyed in Japan. Workers in Sri Lanka might subsequently knit the yarns into panels there, with factories in Hong Kong then link them together to produce the final product. At the other end of the scale, imported high-cost plastic granules would be poured into a moulding machine in Hong Kong; a lever pulled; and out would pop a cheap plastic bucket. Somewhere between these extremes, a shirt would be cut and sewn from cloth woven in Hong Kong from locally spun cotton yarns. Did all these constitute Hong Kong products? If so, why? If not, why not? To complicate matters further still, no internationally established rules of origin existed. Article IX of the GATT required equal treatment for identical products, that is, it is not possible to have one set of origin criteria for country X and another set for country Y. But even this was honoured more in the breach since for imports under preferential arrangements, the GATT often had special qualification criteria. It should be added that these were usually stricter than the country's standard rules of origin. Another consideration was that it was often the type of product as well as its origin that determined which import duty should be paid. For example, an item containing silk entering the UK had to pay a much higher duty than one that did not. Similarly, in the USA an embroidered garment paid a higher duty than one that was not.

By 1960, Hong Kong was exporting to over eighty different markets, each potentially with its own set of origin rules. The government decided that the best way to bring these various issues together was to start from first principles and set down rules of origin that would try to be all things to all people. This was somewhat revolutionary. Normally, an importing country decided what criteria it would use to determine country of origin. A country that was keen to expand its exports might be tempted to interpret such terms as 'substantive transformation' and 'principal processes of manufacture' generously; a country trying to keep imports down might interpret the same words strictly to make it very difficult for unwelcome suppliers to export. Hong Kong turned this on its head by saying, in effect, to its own trade and industry: 'you can get a certificate of Hong Kong origin if you want to export to country X only if you use Hong Kong's rules'. As a result, for some countries, Hong Kong applied stricter rules than an importing country required. Hong Kong took the view that this merely served to reinforce the veracity of its own system.

Hong Kong decided that for agricultural products in their natural state, the country where farmers grew them conferred origin. For fish and other marine life, the port that registered the boat that caught the fish conferred origin. A slight complication arose here in that some fishing vessels were registered both in Hong Kong and in China. In such a case, the location where fishermen landed their catch established origin. For manufactured goods, Hong Kong adopted the principle of substantial transformation. A product could claim Hong Kong origin if it resulted from substantive change in the nature, shape, form or utility of the basic materials used in its manufacture. It added the rider that the product must have undergone the principal processes of manufacture in Hong Kong. Where doubt existed, Hong Kong required a minimum of 25 percent cost content derived from materials and manufacturing activity in Hong Kong, certified by an approved accountancy firm.

Where they required something more than self-certification by the manufacturer, most countries demanded a certificate of origin issued by a chamber of commerce in the exporting country. Since many of these chambers relied for their income on the sale of certificates of origin and offered special prices for their members, clearly, other considerations besides origin criteria might influence their readiness to issue a certificate. It should be pointed out that a Certificate of Origin and a Certificate of Hong Kong Origin differ. The latter certifies specifically that the product has undergone the necessary origin-conferring processes in Hong Kong by companies registered as equipped to make the goods in question. A Certificate of Origin merely certifies the origin claimed for the product by reference to supporting documents. The other certificate-issuing bodies in Hong Kong issued both types. The DC&I issued Certificates of Hong Kong Origin (CHKO) only. When the Hong Kong government stepped in, every Hong Kong factory requiring a certificate of Hong Kong origin had first to register with the Commerce and Industry Department. The department sent inspectors to check that the factory really existed and possessed the necessary plant and equipment to manufacture the goods that required a CHKO. The factory also had to show that it maintained accurate books and records that provided a paper trail which would enable tracing the materials used through the various manufacturing processes in a way that allowed departmental officers to assess whether it had undergone 'substantive transformation' and 'principal manufacturing processes'. Once the DC&I was satisfied on these points, the factory was registered. Each time a registered factory requested a Certificate of Hong Kong Origin, it had to complete an application form which incorporated a declaration that it had made the product in Hong Kong. Any false declaration rendered the factory open to penalties, usually administrative — the refusal of all certificates for three months, which really hurt. They faced severe legal penalties — a fine of $200,000 and imprisonment for two years — but we rarely prosecuted because the Courts took a different view of the importance of our certification. The department then typed the Certificate of Hong Kong Origin. It allowed no erasures or corrections so that inspectors would immediately recognise any altered certificate. Furthermore, for a CHKO, the department required manufacturers to apply two clear working days before the date of shipment in order to allow departmental officers to spot-check the goods to ensure that the shipment was what it purported to be and that all origin criteria had been satisfied. The DC&I spot-checked 10 percent of all applications.

Having dealt with the supply side of the certification process, the DC&I then tackled those at the receiving end. It contacted all overseas governments to explain Hong Kong's rules of origin in detail and the reasons for them. The department circulated the format of the Certificate of Hong Kong Origin and a list of authorised signatories to all countries for dissemination to their Customs officers at the point of entry. The Hong Kong government also undertook to investigate any doubtful shipments that an overseas government might bring to its attention and provide a full report thereon. It also undertook, where the facts allowed, to prosecute any wrong-doers. This action by the government provoked an immediate and satisfactory response from overseas. It convinced governments of the reliability of a government Certificate of Hong Kong Origin. On the downside, many countries insisted that their importers present government Certificates of Hong Kong Origin only. It left the chambers of commerce and trade associations in Hong Kong in a spot because they relied on certification fees for much of their income. The DC&I addressed this problem by setting up a Certification Co-ordination Committee in 1963 that it chaired with members representing the five leading certificate-issuing bodies in Hong Kong: the Hong Kong General Chamber of Commerce, the Chinese General Chamber of Commerce, the Indian Chamber of Commerce, the Chinese Manufacturers Association and the Federation of Hong Kong Industries. Following discussions, it was agreed that the trade and industry bodies, known as GACOS, Government Approved Certificate of Origin Suppliers, would only issue a Certificate of Hong Kong Origin for goods made in factories registered with the DC&I; that they would adhere to the same origin criteria as the DC&I and that they would employ inspectors to carry out spot-checks on consignments. In exchange, the Hong Kong government would designate the five organisations as competent to issue the Certificate of Hong Kong Origin under Section 11 of the International Convention for the Simplification of Customs Formalities 1923. The significance of this was that the GACOS could now issue certificates that were guaranteed by the Hong Kong government. The DC&I was happy to do this for good reason — the volume of applications for certificates was growing rapidly. The department was already bursting at the seams with typists churning out faultless certificates virtually non-stop eight hours a day, five-and-a-half days a week. The six entities providing certificates now shared the task, easing the work-load considerably. Finally, in order not to compromise the system that Hong Kong had devised, but to facilitate trade where it adopted more restrictive origin criteria than those of the importing country, the DC&I subsequently introduced a Certificate of Processing that detailed the precise processes that the product had undergone. The importing country would then decide whether it would accept the shipment as a Hong Kong product.

The government's involvement in certification of origin had an interesting subsidiary impact on the world of philately, of all things. The Hong Kong government took the view that if it was to provide a service for trade and industry that facilitated trade in the way Certificates of Origin of all kinds undoubtedly did, it was only right that those using the service should pay for it rather than the tax-payer at large. It was an expensive service to run even with the low labour costs of Hong Kong, especially as all certificates were typed by hand. At the same time, the government was reluctant to set up a whole new system of shroffs and collection points, recording and issuing receipts for certificate fees. It solved this problem by requiring all applications to carry postage stamps equal to the value of the CO fee. The post office issued a new high-value Hong Kong stamp and kept separate records of their sale. Since few if any postal items required such heavy postage, the amount collected from their sale was offset against the cost of providing the certification service. In this way, the manufacturer or exporter paid for his certificate over the post office counter, thus, avoiding the expensive bureaucracy it would have otherwise involved.

As to goods imported into the territory, Hong Kong's approach to checking origin was rather more simple. It was based on the principle that an item was imported only because someone wanted it or because it was going to be

re-exported. There were no import duties to be paid or considerations of protecting domestic industries, so why worry where the goods came from? Hong
Kong sought only to have reliable import statistics.

The system was well-established by 1963 when I joined the Certification of
Origin Section. A year later, I was promoted to Trade Officer and put in charge
of the Certification Branch, which issued certificates of all kinds. When I was
in charge of certification of origin, we became so concerned about accusations
that Hong Kong passed off other countries' goods that we refused to issue certificates of origin for goods claiming to be 'Designed in Paris' or 'Manhattan
Style' on grounds this might mislead. Ironically, many years later, after I had left
the government, I faced a similar problem the other way round. Our knitwear
factory just outside Canton was making sweaters for the US market but added
the labels 'Made in China' in Hong Kong. An alert DC&I inspector picked this
up and we had a hard time persuading the department that we were not passing
off Hong Kong goods as of Chinese origin. (Our US chain store customer
required special size and colour assortments, and we could more efficiently fill
their orders and add the labelling in Hong Kong in front of the buyer.) In the
1960s, we also took the first tentative steps against misleading brand names.
Some local companies were seemingly surprised to learn that the public might
be confused by such innovative names as 'Coldgate Toothpaste', 'Van Houston
Shirts' and 'Tootloo' ties and cravats.

The Certificate of Hong Kong Origin provided a sound foundation for Hong
Kong's export growth. Though challenging in terms of devising and running
the system and onerous in regard to applying for certificates, it was in its effect
a very successful trade development tool, going a long way to quieten claims of
mislabelling, and persuading people, at last, of the authenticity of Hong Kong
products.

Meanwhile, market forces were busily defining the structure of Hong
Kong industry, determining the type of product it could make while causing a
number of other problems.

By the mid-1960s, Hong Kong had become an established manufacturing centre exporting to over one hundred countries — mainly to the United
Kingdom, Western Europe and North America. Everybody seemed to be
jumping on the band-wagon and business was booming. As quality improved,
British Home Stores in the UK (now Bhs) became the first to take the bold step
of having its goods marked 'Made in Hong Kong' instead of 'Empire Made'. At
this stage, a difference of opinion on trade and industry affairs on the issue of

diversification emerged between the government on the one hand and manufacturing industry on the other. Voices in the government began to argue that the boom could not last. All Hong Kong was doing, they said, was operating as one big production facility. There was nothing original about a Hong Kong product. Rather, the importing country would send a product to Hong Kong to be copied, or 'adapted' as the buyers liked to put it. The Hong Kong factory would quickly manufacture a better and cheaper prototype, customers would place orders and thousands of like articles would roll off the production line. Other Hong Kong factories, seeing the success of the product, would copy the copy and export thousands more at a cheaper price still. The government kept warning that this could not last and urged diversification into new products, designed and developed in Hong Kong by Hong Kong. A succession of Governors in plumed hats, opening the Chinese Manufacturers Association Annual Exhibition of Hong Kong Products in the 1950s and 1960s, would make stirring speeches (drafted in DC&I) about the need for Hong Kong to look to the future, to broaden its industrial base and to embrace up-market designs and enhance the quality of its products. They had in mind to follow the unutterable and ultimate heresy: 'Just like Singapore'. Hong Kong's industrialists listened politely, nodded their heads understandingly, pointed to their bank balances and continued to supply the market with what it asked for.

'There's a difference between being an entrepreneur and a risk-taker', a seasoned Shanghainese multimillionaire manufacturer told me.

The Hong Kong exhortations to diversify were off-beam for four major reasons. The first was space. Hong Kong had not got enough. Most of the territory is sea surrounding 237 islands, largely made up of hills of various shapes and sizes. Whatever flat land existed, had, by the late 1950s, to meet the contrasting and conflicting needs of industry, trade, commerce, banking, farming (in the New Territories), fishing, roads, port facilities, public transport, an airport, bases for the Royal Navy and Royal Air Force and, finally, places for people to live. It became all a bit of a squeeze for the three million people that had to share it. Industry had no particular area it could call home, having to make do with unsafe hillsides, doubtful tenement buildings or expensive purpose-built premises which only the very best could afford. Skywards seemed the only place with plenty of room. Once more, the problem called for government involvement. Enter the flatted factory, a six-storey utilitarian building with each floor divided into individual units, available for rent singly or jointly depending on space needs. It provided a safe and secure home for the small factory and served partially to solve the problem of space. Although the flatted factories marked an obvious advance on a makeshift shack precariously perched on some hillside, still, they were built with public money, mass-produced and one-size-fits-all. This meant that while all floors were load-bearing in terms of machinery and equipment, those factories on the higher floors were more restricted as regards the machinery they could use. Then, factories faced issues of what and how much they could transport in the lift. Further, with limited space, individual manufacturers encountered difficulties in deciding how to divide their floor space between production and storage. The wide common stairways offered a tempting alternative as a dumping ground for any overspill of raw materials. Constant confrontations with the Fire Services Department erupted concerning emergency evacuation of the building, combustibility of goods not contained behind closed fire-doors and overloading of the electrical supply. At the same time, the government undertook a massive reclamation within the far reaches of the harbour. It lopped off the tops of the hills in east Kowloon and dumped them into the sea, creating a large new industrial area, today's Kwun Tong. The government assigned DC&I the task of marketing the land to industry at five dollars a square foot. At first, not many manufacturers expressed interest; factories, of necessity, had become accustomed to manufacturing in the most insalubrious and unbelievable places. In turn, the lack of space created the second problem. Some industries, by their very nature, require sizeable quantities of flat land. No room existed for them in Hong Kong, resulting in the unavailability locally of the raw materials that land-hungry industries tend to produce, thus, the need to import them. In any case, local industry demanded a diverse array of raw materials and it seemed doubtful whether a viable market existed in which heavy industry could survive. Imported raw materials offered a much wider choice. The location of his major customers several thousand miles away in Europe or the United States caused the third problem for the manufacturer.

These three problems conditioned what Hong Kong could make. It was limited to producing relatively small consumer products that could be manufactured in high-rise factories, were labour-intensive to take advantage of low wages, with the added social benefit of providing jobs for many; sufficiently robust to stand up to the handling involved in transporting them several thousand miles across the world; appropriately sized to maximise the consignment and minimise freight charges, competitively priced, and, finally, backed by assurances that they really were Hong Kong products. The fourth reason why the Hong Kong government was wrong to urge change was that Hong Kong was indubitably supplying what its customers wanted. There was no sensible answer to that.

As an aside, it is interesting to note that when China opened up in the late seventies and early eighties, and Hong Kong companies were making massive investments across the border, they continued to manufacture the same goods they had made previously in Hong Kong. This was the business they knew well, the demand was there, so why change?

Manufacturing industries' polite disregard of government advice and the government's reluctant acknowledgement that the businessman knew better than the bureaucrat what was best for him, resulted in a lot of exports concentrated in a fairly narrow range of light industrial products, easily transportable over long distances, and, thankfully, pleasing to the end-consumer. Such goods were not so popular with the domestic producers they were replacing in the importing countries. Lobbies in the developed countries turned up the volume on their protestations about 'sweatshops' and 'low wages' as well as 'fair trade' and 'level playing fields'. In contrast, developing countries, seeking to improve their economies, at the same time, clamoured for 'special and differential treatment' by developed countries, and fell into the embraces of assorted United Nations agencies and international organisations, monetary funds, world banks and quangos all with their considered views on how developing economies should develop. The concept of 'import substitution', the idea that a country should make a product itself instead of importing it, proved especially seductive. Not for the first time, Hong Kong found itself caught between the two, a lone voice seeking to maintain that it was right in the way it did things, and everyone else was wrong. The problem with 'fair trade' is deciding what is fair and who is to be the judge. The trouble with the 'level playing field' is that logically it brings everyone down to the level of the least efficient; if it does not, then, it is not level. The fallacy of 'import substitution' is that no one country is totally self-sufficient, which means that someone has to make choices as to what to import and what to substitute. The problem then is who makes the choices? Only the market can do that successfully through the medium of free trade.

It fell to my lot one day to accompany a local manufacturer whose Junk Bay-produced steel bars were suffering from stiff competition from China, to a meeting with Sir John Cowperthwaite, (then just plain Mr.) the Financial Secretary. Sir John was a fierce free-trader who believed the market could solve all problems (and that narrow roads in Kwun Tong would free up more land for factories). The manufacturer explained his plight in some detail, presented impressive charts and projections in support and asked if the FS could help him.

'Of course I can help you. That is what we in government are here for', boomed the FS. 'Go and make something else'.

The Hong Kong government tried to counter the mounting protectionist pressures by urging free trade on a world that was not very receptive to the exhortations of a tiny British colony with no political influence or economic power and one that did not have to elect a president every four years or a prime minister every five. So, it was only a matter of time before something had to give. Hong Kong manufacturers made good use of that time, not least because of the third piece of paper.

Chapter Four
Commonwealth Preference:
The Third Piece of Paper

The United Kingdom market attracted Hong Kong exporters for a number of reasons.

First, there were the opportunities presented by Imperial Preference. At the time of their signing the Ottawa Agreements of 1932, sixty-five countries and territories, ranging from 'Aden and the Federation of South Arabia' to 'Zanzibar', offered each other Imperial Preference. By the time Hong Kong found itself in a position to take advantage of it, the number granting preference had shrunk considerably as independence became the flavour of the international political scene and the MFN principle the order of the day. From Hong Kong's perspective, the United Kingdom offered the only market of any considerable size among those continuing to provide preferential entry for manufactured goods. Secondly, the old, established trading *hongs* in Hong Kong were British in the sense that their founders had originated in the United Kingdom. It was natural therefore that their connections with Britain should be turned to commercial advantage. Thirdly, some UK manufacturers, notably in the textile trade, were interested in sourcing their grey cloth from the cheapest sources, of which Hong Kong, India and Pakistan were three. Fourthly, there were none of the language barriers that hindered Hong Kong's trade initially with other European countries. Finally, there was a significant body of muted opinion that Hong Kong was owed one. The UK had elected to make it a colony one hundred-odd years previously, declined to hand it back when it had the chance at the end of the Second World War and remained nominally responsible for its welfare. Not that Hong Kong ever received a penny in financial aid from the UK; it had to fend for itself. So, the argument ran, access to its market was the least the UK could do for Hong Kong. 'Trade not Aid' was the catchy international political slogan of the time. The catch lay between the lines: 'trade but not too much of it, thank you'.

The Shanghainese spinners and weavers that had arrived in Hong Kong from China and set up their mills had now become well-established and produced the same quality goods that they had supplied previously from Shanghai. This time, they had the added advantage of Imperial Preference. Exports of cotton yarns from Hong Kong for UK weavers in Lancashire and cotton grey cloth for finishing and retail sale or onward sale to garment makers began to outstrip those of all other goods. They could enter the UK freely with the only requirement that they should meet the criteria laid down for securing Imperial Preference, now given the more politically correct nomenclature of Commonwealth Preference.

The Commonwealth Preference Certificate, the key to qualifying for preference, became the third piece of paper on which Hong Kong built its success — at least at the time it mattered.

The Commonwealth Preference Certificate, known as the CPC, for short, and as an E120 in the trade, the number the UK Customs & Excise gave to the form. A UK Customs & Excise booklet, known as Notice 27A, set out lengthy instructions for obtaining a CPC. Although the criteria were tough, the reward was a considerable saving in duty. In many cases, preferential goods could enter the UK duty free. The value of the CPC has to be seen in the context of the tariffs in force around the world at that time. The import duty served as the principal instrument for protecting domestic industries from competing imports. In so far as it concerned the UK, a non-Commonwealth origin product could attract duties of 50 percent or more (and, at that time, an additional purchase tax as high as 60 percent that made such products prohibitively expensive for most consumers). So there was a considerable incentive for Hong Kong's exporters and manufacturers to obtain a CPC. A number of conditions had to be met. Some were close to those that Hong Kong was already using for the issue of Certificates of Hong Kong Origin. Others were more arduous and complicated. An essential requirement involved achieving the 'prescribed percentage Commonwealth content' for a product, for example, 75 percent for field and opera glasses and 50 percent for items such as sports goods, flasks, shoes and sandals, buttons, cutlery, furniture, glassware, hair combs, clocks, hollowware, screws, padlocks, carpets, rubber goods, pins and needles, paints, pens, paper clips, pottery, nail clippers, bags and wallets made of leather or material resembling leather and toys, all of which were of considerable interest to Hong Kong, and illustrate the wide range of goods that was being manufactured in the territory. What leapt off the page for Hong Kong's manufacturers however was the 25 percent required for 'all other manufactured goods'. For there, off-balance-sheet as it were, lurked yarns, fabrics and garments, the products that later became Hong Kong's largest exports and the source of many problems.

The challenge was how to achieve the required Commonwealth cost content percentages given Hong Kong's free port status and lack of indigenous raw materials. For the essence of the CPC scheme was that, to qualify, a manufacturer had to declare that he had not only made the product in Hong Kong, but achieved the prescribed cost content by using a combination of Commonwealth raw materials, Hong Kong labour inputs and factory overheads, and shipped it directly to the UK. The dilemma for the Hong Kong manufacturer was whether to buy his raw materials at a higher price from Commonwealth suppliers to increase his contribution to Commonwealth cost content or opt for the cheapest price regardless of source to enhance the value of the allowable input costs of Hong Kong labour and overheads. Cotton weavers had the advantage of using Hong Kong spun yarns in their cloth if they so wished. Where UK Customs & Excise had doubts as to the validity of the calculations on which manufacturers based the claim to preference, they could demand cost accounts in a prescribed format from them in order to substantiate it. Though daunting, the rewards of the system in terms of duty advantage made it an attractive proposition.

The true significance of the opportunities arising from the CPC system was that the United Kingdom became, in effect, Hong Kong's domestic market.

But for some, the arduous conditions and the considerable benefits of the scheme made the temptation to cheat irresistible. With Hong Kong manufacturers renowned for their ability to jump on band-wagons, some inevitably decided that life would be much simpler (and the product cheaper still) if they made the necessary declarations and provided the desired certificate to their buyers, with rather less attention paid to the facts on which they supposedly based it. As the volume of CPCs grew, so the risk of discovery diminished — UK Customs & Excise could not cope with the number of spot checks necessary to ensure an effective policing of the system.

When I had been working in London, our company was always being offered a new product from Hong Kong at three different prices. In ascending order of cost, the cheapest was the product sourced from China; the second, an identical product supplied with a Certificate of Hong Kong Origin and the highest, an identical product accompanied by a Commonwealth Preference Certificate. We always went for the one with the CPC because of the tariff advantage. In my naivety, I saw these prices as options as to source of the product. Only five years later, as officer in charge of Hong Kong certification in DC&I, did I realise that the product originated from the same place and it was the price that provided the option. Clearly, nefarious goings-on abounded. The Hong Kong government became very concerned as a growing number of mis-declarations came to light. Those manufacturers who had gone to the trouble of incurring all the work and expense involved in following the system and securing a genuine CPC were also upset. The UK Government approached the Hong Kong government for assistance through the Colonial Office. When DC&I urged a favourable reaction to the approaches, the senior levels of government were less than enthusiastic. They did not condone the alleged misdemeanours but were reluctant to get further involved in matters which would require detailed examination of a company's costs, thus probing into jealously guarded information within a highly competitive manufacturing industry. The Colonial Office for its part pointed out two things: first, protectionist pressures were mounting in the United Kingdom; secondly, the importance of CPCs to Hong Kong and the unthinkable consequences in the event that the qualifying criteria became so strict as to make it virtually impossible for any company to comply with them. In civil servant language this meant do something or else. Within DC&I, it sowed the first seeds of friction between the 'specialist' Trade Officers and 'generalist' Directorate. The TOs argued in favour of taking over the running of the CPC system; the Directorate opposed it. Jimmy McGregor, a Trade Officer at the time, almost single-handedly pushed the government into changing its mind. He did this by drawing up a workable system of control that involved the use of public accountants with professional constraints requiring them to respect their clients' confidentiality but to act honestly in preparing the cost content accounts. This was much less intrusive into a company's affairs and generally acceptable to the genuine manufacturers who were playing by the rules. The Hong Kong government ultimately had to accept that if industry and trade were to be the basis for Hong Kong's survival and development, then the government would have to be seen as determined to discharge its international obligations and ensure that Hong Kong documentation meant what it said. Too much lay at stake to take any other line.

In 1960, the Commerce and Industry Department became the agents of UK Customs & Excise in Hong Kong, and proceeded rapidly to close stable doors before other horses bolted. Once the DC&I became involved, malpractice virtually disappeared and the CPC became a staple for trade with the UK for a number of years thereafter. It did not finally disappear until 1973 when the United Kingdom had to abandon Commonwealth Preference altogether as part of the price of its membership of the Common Market. The enhanced integrity of the revised CPC system went some way toward countering the increasing number of voices in the United Kingdom's cotton textile industry that had been calling for protection since the mid-1950s. They had used false CPC declarations as a rationale for demanding some action on cotton textile imports from Hong Kong.

With the prospect of a general election on the horizon, UK protectionist lobbies changed tactics and emphasis. They pointed to the volume of imports from Hong Kong (and India and Pakistan, also significant suppliers) and claimed that the UK was accepting more imported cotton textiles per head than any other similar developed country, while others afforded their industries greater protection. They played up the historic role of Lancashire and spoke of the decimation of the UK textile industry. More tellingly, they exploited the fact that there were key marginal parliamentary constituencies in Lancashire whose vote could influence the outcome of the next election. As a consequence, both of the UK's major political parties came up with ideas for dealing with the political impact of market forces. The Labour Party favoured setting up a public buying agency to manage cotton textile imports. The Conservatives refused to introduce quotas on Asian Commonwealth countries (i.e. Hong Kong, India and Pakistan) and favoured 'voluntary' export restraints instead. To its credit, the UK Colonial Office argued strongly against any such action but elections are there to be won. Pressure was brought to bear. In 1959 Hong Kong's cotton spinners and weavers of grey cloth 'volunteered' to limit their exports of yarns and grey piece-goods under the terms of a (Hong Kong) industry-to-(Lancashire) industry agreement until 1962. This, it was said, was to afford the Lancashire cotton industry a breathing space in which to restructure and modernise. The fact that the Hong Kong industry agreed to limit exports of cotton yarns and piece-goods to the UK must be seen in context.

First of all the fact that the Hong Kong industry was volunteering was a fiction: it served as a proxy for the Hong Kong government. Hong Kong had little choice. It was in the process of assimilating over a million new people into about sixty square miles of usable space, and it needed to find shelter and work for them. It received financial aid from no one and was totally reliant on itself for ways to alleviate the situation. It needed to trade to survive. In crude terms, it faced a choice between principle and practice; in cruder terms still, some trade or no trade. If even the mother country seemed willing, for domestic political reasons, to override Hong Kong's real concerns, what price other countries with no such ties taking similar action? Hong Kong harboured little doubt that the UK would have its way ultimately. Optimists within the government consoled themselves with the thought that restraints would not last long — after all, Lancashire only wanted a breathing space so the mills could regroup economically. Those in the industry appeared less sanguine. They saw the political reality — one UK party wanted to hold on to power in a number of marginal constituencies; the other wanted to win them over. For them, the practical trade reality consisted of a choice between export control and a UK-based central buying agency.

India and Pakistan volunteered to restrain their exports as well. It was the thin end of a far-reaching wedge for the importing demandeurs and the exporting volunteers. The voluntary agreements became the touch-paper for restrictions on textiles in various formats and with much wider coverage that were to spread across the globe and last for almost another fifty years. That's some deep breath. Underlying the decision taken by Hong Kong, India and Pakistan was an even more significant and highly dangerous issue for international trade. This arose from the interpretation given to Article XIX of the GATT.

Article XIX of the GATT is a masterpiece of that obfuscation that emerges in international negotiations when divergent interests all need to be able to claim that they have achieved their goals. It says in part 'If, as a result of unforeseen developments and the effect of the obligations incurred by a contracting party [i.e. GATT member] under this Agreement, ... any product is being imported into the territory of a contracting party in such increased quantities and under such conditions as to cause or threaten serious injury to domestic producers in that territory of like or directly competitive products, the contracting party shall be free, in respect of such product, and to the extent and for such time as may be necessary to prevent or remedy such injury, to suspend the obligation in whole or in part ...'. This wording presented several problems (besides unscrambling the text) in the late 1950s. What was the measure of 'serious industry'? When was it 'caused'? How to establish when 'serious injury' was 'threatened'? Who determined the time needed to 'prevent or remedy' the injury? And so on. The biggest problem of all was whether the suspension of the obligation to provide MFN treatment was to apply in respect of the principal supplier(s) of the injurious product or to all suppliers of the product. One school of thought was that Article XIX could be used selectively, that is against individual suppliers. This position rested on the view that since Article XIX did not explicitly stipulate a MFN requirement, this provision did not prevent the suspension of Article I. Those who supported using Article XIX only on a non-discriminatory basis opposed this stance. They argued that a note to a similar clause in the Havana Charter (drawn up to establish the failed ITO and precursor to the GATT) required that action against injurious imports 'must not discriminate against imports from any member country'. To which they added the point that single country restraints were completely at odds with the MFN principle that provided the foundation stone of the GATT.

Furthermore Article XIX has a little sting in its tail. It says in paraphrase that a country contemplating action to deal with injurious imports has to notify the other members of the GATT and consult with those likely to be most affected. According to Article XIX, paragraph 3(a), if no agreement between the country wanting to take the action and those affected by it can be reached, 'the affected … parties shall then be free, not later than ninety days after such action is taken, to suspend … the application to the trade of [the country] taking such action of such substantially equivalent concessions or other obligations under this Agreement …'. In more direct terms this is saying that if a country takes action against injurious imports, those affected by the action can retaliate by plonking some equivalent restrictions on the country taking the restrictive action. In fact, the debate on these questions continued for many years. It was to raise its head again with a vengeance in the first half of the 1960s. The danger for Hong Kong of the selective use of Article XIX is obvious. With no political or economic clout, Hong Kong would be at the mercy of any country that wanted to take action against the territory. Nor would it be limited to cotton textiles. Retaliation was not an option for Hong Kong. It would be pointless to restrict imports when they were only imported in the first place because someone needed them.

One cannot but admire the flexibility of the GATT. It is the masterpiece of those who drafted it: an international treaty that no one signed up for but which everyone agreed to follow; requiring all parties to treat each other the same in trade matters, except where they did not have to; and with a safeguard clause that failed to define the circumstances in which it could be used, and, if it were used, could deliver the proverbial ton of bricks, or at least, the suspension of '… substantially equivalent concessions or other obligations under this Agreement …' on whoever tried to implement it. Thanks to its ability to be all things (or nothing!) to all involved in trade affairs, it was not until the completion of the Uruguay Round of Multilateral Trade Negotiations in 1995 that an 'Agreement on Safeguards' was drawn up '… to clarify and reinforce the disciplines of . . . [GATT] Article XIX …'. Until this clarification was finally agreed, rather than protecting a seriously injured or threatened industry in some member country, the 'safeguard clause' as Article XIX was known, served to prevent the world from slipping back into narrow bilateralism because no one was clear how it worked or the consequences if it had been invoked. There was of course one major exception. More of this later.

The underlying uncertainty about Article XIX and the paradoxes that would abound were it to be used, presented Hong Kong and the UK with particular difficulties. The UK and Hong Kong stood as equal members of the GATT except that Hong Kong's membership arose by virtue of its constitutional dependent territory status vis-à-vis the UK. Would the UK really be prepared to test the international waters as to the selective use of Article XIX and limit its action to Hong Kong alone? Given that the UK was responsible internationally for Hong Kong's well-being, could or should it take action that could fatally damage the Colony's economy? And if it did, who would pick up the tab to put things right? And what message would such an act send to others who might fancy taking a pot-shot at Hong Kong? Finally, were selective action to be taken against Hong Kong by the UK, there was no question that under GATT rules Hong Kong was entitled to retaliate. But against the mother country? And to what purpose? And constitutionally, could the Queen command that action should be taken against Hong Kong on behalf of the UK in one breath and countermand her own instructions on behalf of Hong Kong with the next? It is understandable why there were heartfelt sighs of relief all round when the Hong Kong cotton textile industry volunteered to limit its exports of cotton grey cloth and yarns to the United Kingdom.

The sense of relief within DC&I was somewhat muted. It had been clear from the start that the Hong Kong textile industry would not itself be able to operate the industry-to-industry agreement. The potential for conflicts between Shanghainese and Cantonese weavers and among weavers within each of these regional groups would be a certain path to disaster. Then there was the question of who would get how much of the limited amount, and how, and on what basis. The exporters pointed out that it was they who had built up the trade and asked whether it would not be a good idea if they held the quotas. The weavers responded by pointing out that if it had not been for the weavers, the exporters would have had nothing to export. The spinners as yarn producers in their own right and suppliers of the basic raw material to the weavers thought that, if anything, the spinners should hold the quotas. The problem was compounded by language difficulties. The Cantonese and Shanghainese could not understand the other's dialect and the British export houses and bankers could not understand either. Step forward the Commerce and Industry Department once again.

The first thing it did was establish the Cotton Advisory Board (CAB). This had the Director of Commerce and Industry as its Chairman and only Hong Kong government representative. The remainder of the membership was made up of people from the Cantonese, Shanghainese and Brit business communities involved in the cotton industry and trade, including spinners, weavers, dyers and finishers, exporters, and bankers. English was the *lingua franca*. The Director of Commerce and Industry, Ronnie Holmes (later Sir Ronald Holmes), a Brit who had spent the Second World War behind Japanese lines in China and spoke fluent Cantonese, did most of the Cantonese translation. The Shanghainese had a better command of English but it was not until Peter Tsao joined the DC&I that it was able to offer some measure of three-way translation as Peter spoke English, Shanghainese, and Cantonese. The CAB's terms of reference were straightforward: 'To advise the Director of Commerce and Industry on all matters affecting the cotton textile industry'.

The first issue it tackled was how to allocate quotas and to whom and on what basis. At this time (pre-1960), it was still not possible to tell from Hong Kong trade statistics exactly how much yarn had been spun and how much cloth had been woven in Hong Kong and how much of each exported to the UK. After a very brief discussion, engendered by the fact that the longer it went on, the more business was being lost, the CAB advised that the amounts available should be divided on a 50/50 basis between spinners and weavers on the one hand and exporters on the other. Exporters had to show by reference to their books and records (including Commonwealth Preference applications) that they were substantially in the trade with the UK and were awarded quotas on the basis of proven past-performance. This immediately freed up some quantities so that the export trade could resume. Allocating the other 50 percent to spinners and weavers proved more difficult. Manufacturers' books and records at the time were notorious either for their absence or their exaggeration. They provided no basis for an equitable distribution of the quota. In the end, and since the quota was delineated in terms of pounds of yarns and square yards of fabric, it was decided that the number of spindles and looms within each factory would be used to calculate output per factory and that the quota would be allocated proportionate to productive capacity. Once this method of allocation was known to the industry, an incredible range of looms of all shapes and sizes and age were produced for inspection by departmental officers. Some were still in their original Shanghai packing. *Faute de mieux*, this had to do. Using an arcane formula that compensated for looms of different widths and spindles of different whatevers that make them different, quotas were allocated to manufacturers. Fortunately, after a couple of years, a history of past performance was built up and became the basis for future allocations.

This was DC&I's first venture into export controls and almost at once complaints from both sides of the voluntary agreement began to be aired. From the Hong Kong side there was never enough quota to satisfy the orders that came rolling in. Some of the more enterprising weavers, desirous of meeting the needs of their customers, found a way to stretch the amount available. Grey cloth, as its name suggests, is cloth that is unfinished in any way. After weaving, the cloth undergoes other processes such as dyeing and finishing depending on its end use. One aspect of the grey cloth business is the use of temporary marker dyes. The voluntary agreement referred only to grey cloth. Hong Kong manufacturers saw that by dipping their grey cloth in a marker dye, then exporting it as non-grey cloth, they would technically operate both within the law and outside the quota. At the receiving end, the dye could be washed out to leave the grey cloth the importer really needed. Not surprisingly, this ruse annoyed a number of people and added to the complaints from the Lancashire side. Among these was another claim—that Hong Kong was not 'playing the game'. Where once Hong Kong's low prices had been the subject of much criticism from Lancashire weavers who could not compete, the grumbles now were that their prices were too high and directly competing with the top end of the UK market. It seemed not to have occurred to the combined wisdom of the workers, trade unionists and employers of that great mercantile nation that when supply is limited and demand is growing, prices rise. That was not all. It soon became clear that those crafty Hong Kongers were avoiding the restrictions altogether by finishing their own grey cloth and exporting finished piecegoods, which were not subject to restriction. This was therefore threatening the UK finishing industry <u>and</u> the UK weavers of grey cloth who supplied them. The whole agreement had to be reviewed. As a result, the Hong Kong industry volunteered further not to use marker dyes any longer, and agreed that finished piecegoods should also be made subject to restriction. In exchange, the export quota was increased to take account of finished cloth. At the same time, a swing mechanism was introduced. Under this it was possible to use a percentage of the grey cloth quotas for finished piece-goods and vice versa. It set the level at 30 percent and, if this was not enough, it could be increased to no more than 60 percent — known as 'creeping swing'. Immediately, most Hong Kong weavers switched to exporting finished piece-goods because of the higher prices they could get for them. Now, Lancashire screamed not because of too much grey cloth but because they could not get enough. There was just no pleasing some people. The final straw was when some enterprising Hong Kong manufacturers asked themselves the obvious question — if we are weaving fabrics and shipping them to the UK to make into garments, why don't we make the garments ourselves? The first Hong Kong car-coat crossed the oceans, and the Hong Kong garment industry was born, with even more trouble, and not just with the United Kingdom.

Chapter Five
The Comprehensive Certificate of Origin: The Fourth Piece of Paper

Nor was it all sweetness and light several thousand miles away in the other direction.

The Foreign Assets Control Regulations, introduced in 1950, effectively stopped all imports into the United States of America using Chinese raw materials. Although non-discriminatory and applicable to all imports from all sources, it was clear that Hong Kong's emerging industry would be hit harder than most. Consultations were held with the United States with a view to devising a control system that would serve two purposes — to assure the US authorities that a product claiming Hong Kong origin for export there did, in fact, originate in Hong Kong (important for Hong Kong) and to certify that the product contained no materials from the PRC and North Korea (essential for the USA). Establishing Hong Kong origin was not a problem. The USA was happy with the criteria that Hong Kong used. Demonstrating that no Chinese materials had been used in the manufacture of a product was more problematical. USA officials were suspicious. Who could blame them? Hong Kong was on the door-step of China, and its most efficient and busiest port. Hong Kong maintained virtually no surveillance of imports of goods for the reason it did not need any. Hong Kong manufacturers had gained a reputation for ingenuity and sailing close to the wind when irksome controls were in place, and, for many Chinese, their sympathies naturally lay with relatives and friends across the border and their desperate need for foreign exchange. So a whole new control system had to be devised. Each type of product that was exported to the USA had to have its own procedure written up and agreed with the US authorities. The manufacturer then had to undertake to follow it on pain of swingeing fines and two years in jail.

The DC&I was charged with devising and running the system and introduced the Comprehensive Certificate of Origin or CCO, comprehensive in that it certified both product and raw materials. This became the most important of all the certificates issued by the DC&I and the fourth piece of paper to facilitate the growth of Hong Kong's trade and industry.

The procedures meant that any Hong Kong factory that was also registered for ordinary certificates of origin had to segregate any Chinese raw materials used for other markets and place them in a separate store. Often this meant lock-up wire mesh fences on the factory floor with detailed books and records of movements in and out. As with the Commonwealth Preference Certificate, the controls were onerous but the rewards significant, the USA being such a vast market and demand growing rapidly. Some products proved more difficult to control than others. Those in the textile and garment industry, used to the rigours of the Commonwealth Preference system, adapted quickly. Others had much greater difficulty. The ivory and jade carvers presented particular problems. While there were some genuine carvers in Hong Kong who had joined the exodus from China, Hong Kong's trade volumes were such as to suggest that malpractice was taking place, and that Chinese pieces were being passed off as carved in Hong Kong. Since there was an almost insatiable demand from the United States for jade and ivory products—ivory was not then a banned item of trade—some in Hong Kong were always ready to find ways to meet the demand. In so doing they put the whole of Hong Kong's trade with the USA at risk.

I was head of the Certification Branch at the time. In early 1964, a file came across my desk recommending the permanent closure of a jade factory. There was a note pinned to it: — the factory owner wanted to see me personally. I was always wary of such meetings because of the possibility that some corrupt approach might be made. This looked highly suspicious so I arranged that Peter E. I. Lee, Assistant Director, who headed the Controls Division and supervised the Preventive Service, and Jimmy McGregor (my immediate boss) should be present at the meeting. The jade exporter was astonished to find three Brits confronting him. He was very nervous but seemed determined to unburden himself. Peter, Jimmy and I sat and listened as he described how he had refused to participate (further) in the corruption racket that pervaded the CCO procedure for jade and ivory products. He said that he had two genuine jade carvers in Hong Kong but, like others in the business, more orders than he could handle. In order to meet the wishes of his customers in the USA, he paid a regular fee to uniformed officers of the Preventive Service to allow him to smuggle in items from China and pass them off as Hong Kong products.

The standard fee for this dereliction was 2.5 percent of the export price. Peter Lee, who was responsible for the Preventive Service, was shocked. Corruption within certain sections of the government was widely suspected and obviously well known to those who had to pay up. However, efforts to combat it were half-hearted at best. This was because few at the senior levels of the government were willing to believe that corruption existed among British expatriate officers, while those at lower levels were either part of it or unwilling to confront it in the absence of support or encouragement from the top. The situation at the time was likened to a man and a bus: you could be invited to ride on the bus, that is, take part in corrupt activity; walk alongside it, that is, not participate but do nothing; or stand in front of the bus and get run over. Only after the shake-up-wake-up call following the overspill of the Cultural Revolution into Hong Kong in 1967 did the government recognise it had a real problem. Efforts to combat corruption were stepped up and eventually, in 1974, the Independent Commission Against Corruption (ICAC) under Jack Cater was established. Thereafter, several cans of very unpleasant worms were to emerge before the government got its act together and Hong Kong could claim to be clean. The consequence for the DC&I after the jade carver revelations was that a new grade of civilian staff, Industry Officers, was created to work with the Trade Officer Grade where factory visits and inspections were necessary to police trade controls and agreements, a role previously discharged by the Preventive Service.

Once we had established the validity of the jade carver's revelations, we had no choice but to come clean with the US authorities. Things were tense for a while. In the end it was agreed that Hong Kong's genuine carvers should be corralled in communal workshops and closely supervised and that uniformed officers would no longer be used for spot checks. The most irksome condition on which the US insisted was that every consignment destined for the USA had to pass through a central point before loading, and be examined and sealed by a Trade Officer before despatch. This was a massive imposition for hundreds of innocent manufacturers and a set-back for the growing reputation of the DC&I. But it saved the trade. The lower deck of the newly constructed Ocean Terminal became the central point through which all goods had to pass. Only after US confidence in the departmental control systems had been restored a couple of years later was the sealing of individual consignments discontinued. The area is now the home of Toys 'R Us. I was given the task of reviewing all the various CCO procedures and to establish a standard core procedure to which any requirement specific to a product or industry could be bolted on. One product proved particularly difficult and had to have a procedure of its own.

Harvey Levy, the Foreign Assets Control representative stationed in Hong Kong, called on me formally one day to announce that the USA had a serious problem. He had received an urgent telegram from Washington instructing him to express the concern of his government over the number of preserved ducks entering the United States of America. Foreign Assets Control people had been closely monitoring imports. Intelligence reports, statistical analysis, and calculations of available arable land for ducks in the British Crown Colony, had lead them to believe that the volume at which these ducks were entering the United States could only mean that some or more originated in China, contrary to FAC regulations and the agreement between the FAC and the DC&I on the certification procedure for preserved ducks. I admit to having a fleeting image of long lines of ducks, all remarkably well-preserved, originating in China, waddling through the numerous entry-points of the USA in such numbers as to overwhelm the combined defences of the CIA (intelligence), the several bodies that collected statistics (analysis) and the Customs Bureau (products border control), threatening to undermine the very foundations of that bastion of anti-communism. But we were smart enough to realise that we had to give serious attention to the USA's concerns. Apparently, someone in Washington had calculated that the total of disjointed wings, webbed feet, gizzards, etc., exceeded the number of whole ducks that could provide them. This suggested that spare parts of Chinese origin were being added, in contravention of the agreed procedures. Having assured the FAC representative that Hong Kong valued this trade, we set about investigating it. I visited a duck farm in the New Territories to get some first hand knowledge of the business. My interview with the farmer went along the following lines.

'Where do your ducks come from', I asked.

'Eggs', replied the farmer, helpfully, through the Assistant Trade Officer accompanying me as interpreter.

'I mean which country'?

'Ducks for places other than the USA come from China. Ducks for the USA come only from Hong Kong'.

'How can you tell the difference'?

'I paint all Hong Kong eggs red. This is a sign they come from Hong Kong'.

'And how do you distinguish between them when the ducklings emerge from their shells'?

'I put the Hong Kong ones in the special duck pen over there'.

The farmer pointed across the yard to a small wire compound.

'But there are none there', I pointed out.

'They are all preserved', said the farmer.

I was persuaded that the USA had grounds for concern.

The new procedure agreed with the US Foreign Assets Control serves as an extreme example of the lengths we were prepared to go to in order to preserve not only ducks but our burgeoning trade with the USA. This was CCO procedure number twenty-four (implying, correctly, that there were twenty-three other CCO procedures preceding it, and suggesting, again correctly, there were others that followed it). The new scheme involved officers from the Urban Services Department, the Medical and Health Department and the Department of Agriculture and Forestry under the supervisory authority of a Senior Veterinary Officer. The whole system was operated and policed by the DC&I. We had become immune to the nonsense that followed. None of the other departments was particularly amused. Their preserved duck bailiwick covered 'all parts of Hong Kong, Kowloon, the New Territories, and [236] outlying islands, including Lantao.'

Using my contacts in the Trade Officer Grade Association, I have been able to piece together the bizarre arrangements we brought into force some fifty years ago.

First, the producer had to undertake not to buy, sell, import, export, store or otherwise deal in ducklings/ducks or duck parts, preserved or otherwise, of China (PRC) or North Korean origin. At no time could any of the processes involved in the production, packing or storing of preserved ducks or duck parts take place anywhere than in the registered premises. All exports of preserved ducks or parts produced in the registered premises to any destination had to be supported by one or other of the certificates of origin issued by the DC&I. None could be sold locally without the prior written permission of the Commerce and Industry Department. (We did get a letter asking for permission to sell two web feet to Uncle Wong in Central Market but we dismissed this as someone having a (hysterical?) laugh). All ducks had to be leg-banded under the supervision of an officer of the Agriculture and Forestry Department, with each new batch registered with the Department. On receipt from the hatcheries, each batch of ducklings had to be allocated a batch number, and different batches had to be 'totally segregated from each other, from the moment of receipt from the hatcheries onward.' Clear identification markings had to be maintained in such a manner as to enable inspecting officers to determine the batch number of any particular batch. (I have a mental picture of a duck parade and roll-call every morning.) The procedure insisted in the strongest possible way that 'leg-banded ducks will not under any circumstances be slaughtered or otherwise disposed of, nor will leg-bands be removed except under the supervision of an officer of the responsible department concerned'. Not only that, all ducks to be processed had to be inspected ante-mortem and post-mortem. Requests for such inspection had to be made in writing to the department concerned at least three days in advance of the date of the desired inspection and batch numbers and actual numbers of ducks to be inspected had to be stated. (The scenario gets even more bizarre — Did the chilling whisper go round the selected batch of ducks, 'Pssst! The dreaded letter of request for inspection has gone in . . .'). Seven days were allowed from the slaughter of the ducks for processing and packing and any ducks processed outside of this period could not qualify for certification. Processed ducks had to be packed in consumer packages bearing a label printed in English showing:

'i   The name of the product
ii The name of the country of origin preceded by the words 'Product of ....' which statement shall appear immediately under the name of the product
iii The word 'Ingredients' followed by a list of the ingredients in the case of the product being fabricated from two or more ingredients including a declaration of artificial flavourings or preservatives
iv The name and place of business of the manufacturer or distributor qualified by a phrase that reveals the connection that such a person has with the product
v An accurate statement of the quantity of the product'

All shipments had to be routed through the Kowloon Inspection Control Centre in the Ocean Terminal. Perhaps, the most extreme measure was that a monthly return had to be prepared by an accountant approved by the department, and 'submitted to the Commerce and Industry Department by the 15th of the month following that under review'. The return had to give the following information:

'i   Opening stock of ducks and/or ducklings and batch numbers
ii Opening stock of semi-processed and processed ducks or duck-parts by description, quantity, weight and batch numbers

iii Number of ducks slaughtered and the quantity of ducks and duck-parts processed by description, weight and batch numbers

iv Details of duck and duckling losses giving reasons and indicating batch numbers as appropriate

v Sales by description, quantity and weight and batch numbers, quoting the names and addresses of both consignees and exporters. The reference number of the relative Comprehensive Certificate of Origin and other certificates must be quoted.

vi Closing stocks of live ducks'

In order to provide a basis for the accountant's return, the producer had to maintain Form PD/6 showing that the total number of parts of ducks equalled exactly the number of whole ducks used to produce the individual parts. This was designed to ensure that no spare legs, wings, etc, were slipped into the shipment at the last minute. The formula was very clear: one duck = two wings = two legs = two webbed feet and so on. As I recall, a duck was deemed to comprise seventeen separate parts as listed in the form. Legs and wings were counted as two pieces and not one pair. (We had been surprised to learn that virtually everything the poor duck possessed was considered edible and in some cases highly prized. There were some minor disputes over the actual number of edible parts. These were resolved by listing the seventeen different parts on the form that everyone could agree on and ignoring anything else.) Any deliberate breach of these conditions rendered the offenders liable to a fine of $100,000 and imprisonment for two years. These swingeing penalties had been included in the original legislation as an indication to overseas governments of Hong Kong's determination to uphold the integrity of its certification systems and as a warning to potential offenders. The Courts, which had the final say when proceedings were taken, usually fined the guilty ten dollars and told them not to do it again.) Any questions concerning these arrangements, and one can imagine there were many, could be addressed to the Assistant Trade Officer (Preserved Ducks) at a given telephone number. (This became known as the PD hotline.)

Unlike the edicts of the Qing Dynasty, the Notice to Exporters did not conclude 'Tremble and Obey,' but it did have the desired effect of demonstrating the Hong Kong government's willingness to respond positively to the wishes of other governments, and of providing a satisfactory tool with which the US administration could defend itself against further threats from China, at least so far as preserved ducks were concerned.

Whether any Hong Kong farmer ever complied (or even understood) any of this is doubtful but somehow the trade survived and more importantly so did our much more important other trade with the USA. Only in later years, when Hong Kong's exports to the United States were on a massive scale and the US had become Hong Kong's largest market, did we fully appreciate how close we had come to jeopardising the whole trade because of the acts of a few corrupt officers, jade carvers and duck farmers.

The Comprehensive Certificate of Origin and the procedures devised to support its veracity, the fourth piece of paper, understandably played an essential part in the development of Hong Kong's trade with the USA.

In 1967, I was promoted to Senior Trade Officer and posted to the industry side of the Commerce and Industry Department. This coincided with another tough time for Hong Kong industry. For once the problems arose not overseas, but locally. May of that year saw the first manifestations of the overspill of China's Cultural Revolution in Hong Kong. Protesters assembled in Garden Road outside the Hong Kong Hilton Hotel. Little red books were thrust into the air accompanied by strident shouts in support of Chairman Mao or to denounce the British administration. The unrest soon spread throughout the colony, causing much disruption to everyday life. Strikes by bus drivers made communications within the territory difficult. Things turned ugly. Lam Bun, a well known radio personality, was murdered and several people, including the Police Force's bomb-disposal expert, were mutilated by explosive devices of various kinds planted in the streets. The old Bank of China Building was festooned with full length, large-character slogans while blaring loudspeakers on the outside of the building purveyed anti-British slogans and the thoughts of Chairman Mao to passers-by. Business was severely disrupted. The government was caught off-guard. Many prominent local and overseas personalities discovered they had pressing engagements the other side of the world. Only the Police Force seemed to know how to react. It dealt with riots and ugly demonstrations in various parts of the colony in exemplary fashion and earned considerable praise from those members of the public who did not side with the rioters. The Queen later conferred the title 'Royal' on the Force. An expat businessman conceived the idea of establishing a trust fund whereby those who supported the police's action could make donations to be used for the education of the children of low-paid police officers. He asked the government for help to run it. The DC&I was called in. Presumably the thinking was—ah, businessman; must be DC&I. Whatever the reasoning, the result was that DC&I became overnight a centre of counter-propaganda. For reasons never made known to me — expendable perhaps — I was charged with collecting donations to the Police Fund. This was no ordinary collection system and no ordinary collection point. A desk was strategically placed at the corner of the L-shaped corridor on the third floor of Fire Brigade Building. Donors could approach the desk either by the main staircase—by using the staircase a potential donor could be visiting any of the department's offices open to the public—or the lift, which was programmed to stop at every floor so that anyone planted by the opposition to keep a check on who was doing what could not be sure at which floor lift-users disembarked. The third floor housed the departmental registries and the directorate offices so only known departmental staff and donors used it. The desk was positioned some distance from the lift. I therefore had a good view of who was approaching. Just to be sure I had a loaded revolver in the top right-hand drawer of my desk. The wisdom of such placement was, fortunately, never put to the test — I am left-handed and my only firearms experience was limited to discharging an Enfield 303 many years previously during my National Service. The other wing of the corridor led from the desk to a back staircase, used surreptitiously by sundry local big shots and knights of the realm, generous in their donations but modest in their desire for publicity. In order to protect anonymity, receipts were only given if asked for. No one asked. The fund was hugely supported, and I stuffed great bundles of bank-notes into the drawers and cupboard of my desk until another staff member took them off my hands for counting. Donors rarely used cheques, which gave too much away. Each day, we announced the amount collected; never the name of the contributors. Donations were also received by post. A few envelopes contained paper hell-money burnt at funerals, a nice touch on the part of the secular, non-believing, protesters (who claimed that religion was the opiate of the masses but nonetheless called on some mysterious Other to give Chairman Mao ten thousand years of life). The Police Fund proved a powerful and practical way in which those who did not support the rioters could express their dissatisfaction with their antics without necessarily implying admiration for the colonial government that was the target of the rioters' wrath.

The Industry Branch of DC&I was given over to counter propaganda. We composed letters to the editors of Chinese and English language newspapers that did not support the rioters, giving false names and addresses, and posted from various locations around Hong Kong to give the appearance they came from the general public. These praised the Police Force and criticised the acts of the rioters. They claimed that ambulances could not get through to Queen Mary Hospital with the injured and that birds and animals in the Botanical Gardens were starving because the rioters denied access. In retaliation, the press supporting the rioters claimed police brutality; denounced all Chinese working for the government as lackeys and, worse, all Brits as of the porcine persuasion. One paper even accused DC&I's Jimmy McGregor, the scourge of all corrupt officers, of personal corruption. Jimmy McGregor sued the newspaper at the height of the disturbances, and won.If these troubles were not enough, another problem arose, this time, with a natural rather than a man-made cause. It failed to rain. The reservoirs dried up. The whole of Hong Kong was put on water rationing — four hours water, every four days. DC&I joined the Government Emergency Water Supplies Group and went into bat for industry and its essential need for water. The silver linings to these dark but non-rain-bearing clouds were to be found in three unexpected areas. First of all, the rioters failed totally to attract support from the industrial work-force. Attendance at factories reached an all time high, job-hopping decreased and absenteeism became virtually non-existent. The strike by bus workers, more than anything, served to upset worker solidarity. Hong Kong's entrepreneurial spirit came to the fore instead, as anything on wheels was pressed into service, offering rides to wherever you wanted to go for twenty cents. Small vans, in particular, did a roaring trade and gave birth to today's ubiquitous minibus. The second silver lining was, at the time, even more welcome. China, seeing the territory's plight, offered to share its water with Hong Kong. Huge pipes were laid down the centre of Hong Kong's streets and China began pumping water to an unwashed, thirsty, but grateful population. The most unlikely silver lining of all was that the government began to get a grip on things. Opposite the Bank of China stood Beaconsfield House, home of the Information Services Department. Loudspeakers were attached to its walls and Cantonese opera played at full volume, drowning out the offerings from across the road. The savings book of the Hong Kong and Shanghai Bank was encased in a red plastic cover and closely resembled the book of Chairman Mao's thoughts. It was a useful weapon with which to counter the chanters and thrusters on the streets, although circumspection was advisable as to when and where such satire might be exercised. The unrest slowly died down. Changes were introduced by the government to make it more user-friendly and in touch with the governed. The Colonial Secretary became the Chief Secretary overnight. The Colonial Secretariat became, simply, the Secretariat. Official letters no longer pretended that the writer was the recipient's obedient servant and signed off 'Yours faith-fully' instead. Traditionally all letters had finished with a usually indecipherable signature and the title of the Head of Department, for example, 'for Director of Commerce and Industry'. Now letters were personalised, and signed by a named person using a title describing his or her position in the department. It even gave a telephone number the recipient could call for follow-up purposes. Greater efforts were made to combat corruption.

One incident, perhaps, typifies the stand-off that the Cultural Revolution caused in Hong Kong. Fire Brigade Building no longer exists but used to stand on the waterfront in Central opposite the Yaumatei vehicular ferry. In the fore-court of the ferry, there was a bus terminus. A few local and expatriate staff, including Jimmy McGregor and I, were still working in the department one Saturday afternoon trying to sort out how to apportion water supplies among competing industries. A loud commotion was heard outside in the street and traffic came to a halt. A chanting mass of bus drivers and Red Guard look-alikes waving their Little Red Books were pointing at the building and making demands that were hard to understand in the cacophony of noise that greeted each exhortation from the leader. Someone was sent down to check that the solid teak doors to the building were securely bolted and seemingly designed to resist more than shouts and slogans. It was now ten to six in the evening, and the crowd was getting restless. The remaining staff were assembled in the conference room and it was established that the mob was demanding that the Union flag on the roof should be taken down. The police were contacted by tel-ephone and they promised to send a platoon as soon as one became available. Jimmy McGregor sent me up on the roof with my instructions. The flag-pole, situated at the very front of the building, overlooked the people below. When the crowd saw me, the shouting and boos intensified. I checked my watch, walked to the pole and undid the ropes. The crowd sensed what was happen-ing. The jeering and booing turned to ringing cheers and delighted laughter. The flag was coming down. Those of the porcine persuasion had suffered another humiliating defeat. All power to the thoughts of Chairman Mao! And of course, to Colonial Regulations that required the lowering of all Union flags on public buildings at six o'clock precisely each evening.

Chapter Six
The Arrangement that Lived Up to Its Name

I have already described how, in 1958, the Hong Kong textile industry was persuaded to volunteer restraints on its exports of cotton yarns and grey piecegoods to the United Kingdom, and how, shortly thereafter, it was further persuaded to volunteer additional restrictions on finished fabrics. I also pointed to the move up-stream that Hong Kong manufacturers were to make into garments. I have mentioned also the increasing interest the USA showed in Hong Kong products and that the US market attracted Hong Kong because of its size and the long production runs that large orders made possible. Hong Kong quickly built a presence for its products in the USA, especially garments. Protectionist elements raised the alarm, that is to say, their alarm, trotted out the usual cries of 'floods of imports' and 'fair trade', among others, to the extent that friendly Senators and Representatives began to get worried about their future careers in Congress if they did not do something about it. In 1960, President Kennedy had made an election promise to textile interests to take action against 'rising imports' of 'cotton textiles and apparel' to the USA. In fulfilment of that promise, he invited developed and developing countries to agree that the time was ripe for an international short-term arrangement 'to bring some order' to international trade in cotton textiles. Developing countries were encouraged to sign up when the much-respected president pointed to an obscure part of the US Agricultural Act, Section 204, passed in 1956, which empowered him to 'negotiate' with exporting countries and impose restrictions on imports of textile products. The choices boiled down to three: imposed restrictions, a negotiated 'voluntary' bilateral agreement with the USA or an agreement covered by a pseudo-legal derogation from the GATT's basic principle of non-discrimination. All of these were seen as preferable to the complexities that could arise from the use of GATT Article XIX. The president's invitation was one that other developed countries were more than happy to go along with. They, too, were either being 'flooded with imports' or feared they would be through 'diversion'.

'Diversion' as a reason for restrictions on trade, has not appeared in this story so far. It constitutes another of those 'fair trade', 'level playing field' catch phrases that have the semblance of reason but do not stand up to close examination. 'Diversion' is the argument that if a country with significant imports of a particular item, closes its doors to that item, the suppliers who are shut out will promptly switch their shipments to some other market, thus causing problems for that new market. As any businessman will tell you, business does not work quite like that. There are such considerations as finding a buyer in a market you have yet to enter, securing an order, and understanding which products, what styles, which colours, what packing and what sizes, are appropriate for that market and how sizes are measured in it. Then there is the question of what tariffs apply to what goods, and how easy or difficult it is to move goods from factory to consumer. Such niceties however are not allowed to stand in the way of a country or a politician that wants to appear responsive to the demands of constituents. Nor were they in this case. In 1961, the Short Term Arrangement Regarding International Trade in Cotton Textiles (STA) was born. For once it lived up to its name — within a year it was replaced by the Long Term Arrangement Regarding International Trade in Cotton Textiles (LTA). This was scheduled to last for four years to give those cotton textile industries affected by imports adequate time to adjust. Not surprisingly all those industries were located in developed countries.

As soon as the LTA took effect, countries were queuing up to negotiate with Hong Kong — the USA, Canada, West Germany, the Benelux countries and the Nordics, among others. The special relationship between the UK and Hong Kong became even more farcical. Hong Kong was urged to volunteer once more to extend the coverage of its cotton exports to the UK to include garments. However, this time, the two would meet government to government instead of industry to industry and would pretend that they were dealing with each other at arm's length under the terms of the new STA-cum-LTA. The UK side would be led by someone from the Board of Trade. However, a representative of the Foreign and Commonwealth Office, which until then, had skilfully concealed any understanding of, or support for, the problems of Hong Kong's textile industry, would join the Hong Kong government team to ensure fair play for Hong Kong. Only one of these FCO chaps, Derek Jones, ever showed any real concern for Hong Kong over a series of negotiations, and he finished up some years on as the DC&I's man in Geneva and later as Secretary for

Economic Services, Secretary for the Environment and Secretary for Transport in the Hong Kong government. To make matters worse, it was felt that, for constitutional reasons and because of the UK's metropolitan responsibilities for its dependent territories under the GATT, a UK presence should attend Hong Kong's negotiations with other countries in order to 'assist' Hong Kong and formally approve any arrangements that Hong Kong entered into with other countries. It was not clear who loathed this system most: the UK representative who was the butt of many pointed references to the UK's own position when Hong Kong tried to stand firm on an issue in a negotiation; or the country with which Hong Kong was supposed to be negotiating, who could never be sure if it was talking to Hong Kong's interests or the UK's; or the Hong Kong government, which was reluctant to reveal its negotiating position and the views of its industrial advisors to either of the other parties.

Things came to a head when David Jordan, an acerbic civil servant, first class boss and Hong Kong's Chief Trade Negotiator at the time, felt he was being ordered to agree to something by the leader of the British side. A note had been pushed under his hotel room door during the night to the effect that 'If we cannot meet tonight, you must agree to restraints tomorrow.' At the next morning's session, David Jordan demanded to know who had put the note under his door.

'I did', said the man from the Board of Trade.

'And who are you'? asked David.

'I am the representative of the Board of Trade', was the indignant reply.

'In that case, I have nothing to say to you', said the Hong Kong negotiator. 'I take my instructions from the Queen, through the Governor of Hong Kong, not from some minion from Whitehall', and walked out.

There was a tremendous fuss, but thereafter, no one showed up to represent the FCO in cotton textile negotiations, and any agreement that Hong Kong made after that was passed on the nod by the UK. Some years later in 1982, when I was Chief Trade Negotiator, we were in Geneva at a meeting of the developing countries. On textiles, we found ourselves very much in tune with the position of Argentina on a particular point of importance to Hong Kong and had agreed on a strategy for our separate meetings with the United States team. The same day, Argentina and the UK fell out over the Falklands. I was summoned by the UK Ambassador to the GATT and told that we could have no more dealings with the Argentineans. This cut right across our plans, so, I thought I would use David Jordan's precedent and remind His Excellency that I took my instructions from the Queen through the Governor of Hong Kong.

'I am the Queen', replied the Ambassador, pointing to the framed letters of appointment on his wall.

My sterling defence of Hong Kong's interests resulted in a severe telling-off from the Ambassador in Geneva and the Governor in Hong Kong when I reported back. I took some consolation from the fact that not many people have been told off by two queens on the same day.

Hong Kong finished up with a number of agreements. Exports of cotton textiles were subject to various degrees of restraint under terms agreed upon with the United Kingdom, West Germany, the Benelux countries, Austria and Italy. France continued to ignore Hong Kong and the STA-cum-LTA altogether and kept its illegal import restraints in place as usual. In the Americas, we reached agreements with the USA and Canada. There was also an agreement with Australia. Japan maintained illegal restrictions on imports of silk products from Hong Kong while happy to export to Hong Kong the fabrics from which they were made.

In reaching these agreements, Hong Kong took a different position from the other developing countries that were lined up for restraint action. An annex attached to the STA, continued in the LTA, divided all cotton textiles into sixty-four categories. These supposedly covered all the relevant tariff numbers of items that could be caught under the terms of the Arrangement, provided they were of cotton, that is, 50 percent or more by weight of cotton. In fact, they were taken directly from the US tariff schedules that were used by no one but the USA. While the sixty-four categories set the boundaries for restrictions, the LTA contained two specific articles as to the items to be restrained. The one (Article 3) stated that restraints could be applied only to those particular products from particular sources that were causing or threatening to cause 'market disruption', the particularity presumably being the product being caught within one of the sixty-four categories and meeting the definition of cotton. The other article (Article 4) said that there was nothing to stop two countries finding mutually acceptable arrangements consonant with the LTA and no more restrictive than restraints would be if the product-by-product approach of Article 3 had been used. The USA and some other developed countries pressed the advantages and certainties arising from 'comprehensive' agreements that covered all sixty-four categories but offered generous limits well in excess of trade levels for all but the most 'sensitive' categories.

'Sensitive' is another of those terms of art in trade negotiations. It is supposed to mean those products said to be causing particular concern to the importing country. In practice it meant those products whose industries or lobbyists had the most clout.

Losing out as they were to Hong Kong and being offered enticements by the importing countries of quantities well in excess of their current levels of trade, most of the developing countries signed up for mutually acceptable 'comprehensive' arrangements under Article 4. While these covered all cotton textile exports, they were said (by the importing countries) to offer the developing countries generous margins for growth. Hong Kong took a more principled stance. It argued that restraints were bad for trade. Discriminatory restraints on trade from particular sources were even worse. Nonetheless, having signed up for the LTA, it would honour its obligations to the full. In this regard, it would accept restraints on exports of any product from Hong Kong that could be shown to be causing or threatening to cause problems. It would not accept comprehensive agreements, which by definition, implied either that all products were causing or threatening to cause difficulties, or that some products were not causing or threatening to cause them, and therefore, subject to unnecessary restraint. The United Kingdom set about securing a considerable number of individual restraints on a list of cotton items from Hong Kong. Other European countries followed suit although the coverage of restrictions was not as wide as that of the UK. The USA was aghast at this breaking of ranks in the developed world. It had envisaged a nice cosy arrangement whereby all cotton textiles trade from developing countries would be cocooned in a network of restraints while the developed countries could continue their textile trade with each other without let or hindrance. Hong Kong had thrown a spanner in the works. The great USA was helpless to do anything about it. Having written the rules, it now had to play the game by them. The consequence was that the USA went after Hong Kong in a big way. It began to request 'consultations with a view to reaching a restraint arrangement' on all cotton textile exports from Hong Kong, category by category. Its objective was clear: each of the sixty-four categories in which Hong Kong had any trade, was to be sealed off, one by one, until, to all intents and purposes, Hong Kong would be left with a series of individual category restraints that in total would amount to a comprehensive agreement similar to those the USA had reached with other developing countries.

In 1961 or 1962, a new Administrative Officer, by the name of Philip Haddon-Cave, had been posted to the DC&I as Assistant Director. He proceeded to give the department a good shaking up, much to the concern of his directorate colleagues, the opposition of the senior members of the Trade Officer Grade, and the delight of the junior Trade Officers of which I was one. He reorganised the hitherto mysterious Overseas Trade Relations Branch into two Commercial Relations Divisions, responsible for trade negotiations, and deferred to the tenacity of Jimmy McGregor who insisted on holding on to his Industry Division. Other consequences of his arrival are described later but as far as the USA' s attempt to force Hong Kong into a comprehensive agreement step-by-step, Haddon-Cave struck back with impeccable timing.

Every Hong Kong trade negotiator was taught from birth that since restraints on trade are bad, there was no such thing as a good restraint agreement. Nonetheless, there were some where Hong Kong did not do too badly, and some where it did rather well. This was because Hong Kong teams always did their homework before any trade negotiation and always listened to (and followed) the advice of the Cotton Advisory Board.

As the US drew Hong Kong and the sixty-four categories ever more tightly into its net, Haddon-Cave informed the USA that Hong Kong would be prepared to listen to any proposals the USA might have for a 'comprehensive' cotton textile agreement, provided there were sufficient inducements to persuade Hong Kong that such an agreement was in the mutual interest of the USA and Hong Kong. The USA could not believe its luck and Hong Kong its ears when the USA said 'OK'. Hong Kong had correctly judged that too long a stand on principle could find Hong Kong severely disadvantaged in the USA market with individual product categories encumbered with restrictions of various kinds. There were few categories left where Hong Kong would be able to expand. On the other hand, to lock in the numbers it presently had combined with the sort of flexibility that other countries enjoyed in their comprehensive agreements, would provide Hong Kong with a significant advantage. Trade officers in the DC&I had been beavering away and come up with an interesting statistic: if Hong Kong could secure the current numbers and reasonable flexibility provisions in a comprehensive cotton textile agreement with the USA, Hong Kong's total equivalent square yardage[1] would be greater than that of all other restrained countries put together. In other words, Hong Kong

---

[1]   In order to provide some flexibility in restraint agreements, the possibility existed for some of one category's products to be used to ship goods from another category, say, shirts for trousers. In order to do this, agreed factors converted each item into equivalent square yards of cloth. This common unit could then be used to calculate the total access rights covered by a restraint agreement.

would have cornered the cotton garment market. The advice from the Cotton Advisory Board was direct and to the point: ditch the principle; go for the trade. The Hong Kong team was led by Haddon-Cave. I was a member as the Officer-in-Charge of the Textiles Controls Division. It was a tough negotiation, but following meetings in Hong Kong and another in Washington, a deal was struck and Hong Kong emerged as the world's largest exporter of cotton garments. It did not bruit such news around — other developed countries might want to emulate the USA and other developing countries would find out soon enough. With significant numbers locked away in the new comprehensive cotton agreement with the USA as back-up, Hong Kong manufacturers ventured on their next step to meet the ever growing demand for their garments.

Man-made fibres (mmf) were increasing in popularity as fabrics for use in garments. Cotton and mmf blends were especially popular since they combined the benefits of cotton with the advantages of easy care. The LTA defined a cotton product as one that contained 50 percent or more of cotton by weight or value. Hong Kong manufacturers were soon exporting garments made up of 49 percent cotton, 51 percent man-made fibres. There was worse news still for the USA. Other developing countries, seeing what Hong Kong was doing, soon joined in. Not only that, since they had been bought off early and had very small cotton quotas in comparison with Hong Kong, they began concentrating heavily on exports of blended garments, outpacing even Hong Kong whose principal focus remained on cotton apparel. There was seemingly nothing to be done. The LTA, at USA insistence, had been drawn up to deal with cotton textiles. The apparel now in question was, by definition, not of cotton. A new product had been invented as the market hit back at those who sought to interfere with it. If the US government was not amused, the US textiles lobbies were furious, loudly denouncing Hong Kong manufacturers and others as downright cheats and more. The rule-makers were, again, suffering from the consequences of their own acts.

At the same time, Hong Kong manufacturers were embarking on another step to meet what seemed to be insatiable world demand for garments of all kinds. Despite the fast expanding market for blends, pure cotton garments remained the consumer's first choice. Hong Kong and other major suppliers were already subject to comprehensive restraints. Hong Kong manufacturers went on an investment expedition. Most developing countries in South East Asia were struggling to industrialise. Thanks to such policies as protective tariffs and import substitution, few were succeeding. They were all desperate for overseas investment in new industries that created jobs for their people. What better than garment-making with its low set-up costs, assured markets and high labour content? Manufacturers from Hong Kong were happy to oblige. They identified a number of developing countries that had no or very small garment industries and consequently no restraints on their exports, and moved in. Hong Kong-owned factories sprang up all over the place. Macau, the Philippines, Malaysia, Thailand and Sri Lanka were particularly popular.

Then began a cat and mouse game as importing countries tried to apply restraints on cotton textiles exported from these new sources. This was not easy since the LTA required that imports of such products had to be sufficiently large as to cause serious problems. Since these countries were starting from scratch, at least some trade had to be allowed to build up in order to provide a basis for restraint consultations. It also had to be done on a product by product basis, unless, of course, generous comprehensive agreements were offered instead. As soon as one supplier was restrained so another would pop up somewhere else. The situation became farcical (and even more difficult to control) when the USA and China resumed diplomatic relations. Hong Kong was quick to invest just across the Chinese border. Other Hong Kong manufacturers began investing even farther afield in countries like Portugal and took advantage of favourable investment incentives in such work-starved places as North East England and Ireland, the very countries supposedly suffering from too many garments! It would be going too far to claim that Hong Kong took a key role in launching the industrialisation of South East Asia, but it certainly demonstrated a more practical way to get things moving as an alternative to the theories of the experts that abounded from donor countries and international organisations, with their wildly optimistic projections for economic expansion. (The knitting factory that I joined after taking early retirement from the government had operations in Hong Kong, China, Thailand, Malaysia, the Philippines and Sri Lanka.)

Meanwhile, the problem of cotton/mmf bends would not go away. The USA again made threats and reference to Section 204 of the Agriculture Act. Developing countries needed the exports. Pressures were applied. The advantages of orderly trade and generous growth factors were again dangled before the exporting countries. Malaysia was the first to capitulate. It was offered several million square yards equivalent to volunteer restraint on its exports of man-made fibres to the USA. The amount on offer was much higher than its level of trade. It accepted. The domino effect was repeated as developing countries lined up to volunteer. In their defence, they had little choice: Hong Kong had the cotton quotas sewn up; the other developing countries were big in man-made fibres and wanted to preserve as much of their trade as they could. Hong Kong, meanwhile, ignored all hints and blandishments and kept on shipping. For once, it had the full support of the United Kingdom and some other European countries. They feared that the LTA and another spate of voluntary agreements would undermine the GATT still further, and make it impossible to limit the problem solely to textiles. Once other industries successfully claimed 'me too', all would be lost. The spectre of developed country taking action against developed country raised its unacceptable head. The USA remained unmoved. It kept up the pressure on Hong Kong and sent no less a person than Mr. Maurice Stans, US Secretary of Commerce, and a high-level delegation to smooth-talk Hong Kong's Financial Secretary, John Cowperthwaite. Mr. Stans served as President Nixon's right-hand man and later found fame and misfortune in the Watergate affair. Peter Tsao, the Shanghainese Assistant Trade Officer, who had moved rapidly up the promotion ladder since his gallant efforts at three-way translation in the Cotton Advisory Board, and I were given the task of preparing the brief. We were also present at the fateful encounter. It could not be described as a meeting of minds, and, in some respects, not even as a meeting, for it lasted but a short while. Mr. Stans opened by asking Hong Kong what it wanted.

'Free trade', answered the Financial Secretary. 'You are the demandeurs'.

'I'm not here to play games', snapped the Secretary of Commerce. 'I need an agreement'.

'What Hong Kong needs is free trade in order to survive'. The Financial Secretary pressed on undaunted.

It was all very undiplomatic and Secretary Stans stormed off empty-handed. The next day, the US Consul General in Hong Kong was round at the DC&I warning all and sundry that Mr. Stans was not a man to be trifled with, and that Hong Kong had caused irreparable damage to its standing in US eyes. Then the truth emerged. President Nixon wanted to get re-elected. Certain promises had been made to the US textiles lobbies. Nothing was more important in the President's eyes than the President getting re-elected. Article XXII of the GATT requires a member to 'accord sympathetic consideration to, … and adequate opportunity for consultation regarding such representations as may be made by another contracting party with respect to any matter affecting the operation of [the GATT]'. The Cotton Advisory Board thought that Hong Kong would put itself in a false position if it refused point-blank to hold further consultations. Using the hook of Article XXII, therefore, Hong Kong went fishing. By this time, some changes had taken place in the department. Jack Cater was now Director of Commerce and Industry, and Bill Dorward, by now an Assistant Director of Commerce and Industry promoted from the Trade Officer Grade and acting Acting Chief Trade Negotiator, had been replaced by Eric Ho, from the Administrative Grade. The Cotton Advisory Board had become the Textiles Advisory Board or TEXTAB, for short. Several rounds of consultations were held in Hong Kong and Washington without any real progress. The USA wanted Hong Kong to volunteer just as it had for the UK some years before. Hong Kong argued that the LTA had been the instrument that was supposedly and at US insistence designed to deal with the problems of the US textile industry.

'A shirt is a shirt is a shirt', said the USA.

'If you are saying that Hong Kong can use its cotton and blends quantities interchangeably, we might be prepared to listen', responded Eric Ho. The USA never mentioned the shirt argument again.

The full TEXTAB travelled to the USA for what turned out to be the last round of talks. By this time, I had reached the rank of Assistant Director of Commerce and Industry, and was in charge of Hong Kong's commercial relations with Europe. It was only natural, therefore, that I should be dragged into the Hong Kong/US textile negotiations — natural, because that is the way governments work. The consultations were held in the State Department in Washington. They were tough and, sometimes, acrimonious. The Hong Kong team was gallantly led by Eric Ho. He had to juggle with a ruthless president determined to get re-elected, frequent telephone calls from the UK government urging Hong Kong not to concede, a Financial Secretary who believed in free trade and a Hong Kong Governor who had to try to please everybody. A nervous TEXTAB back in the Watergate Hotel who thought its business was going down the drain, was kept informed of developments by Jack Cater who was briefed every hour, The urgings from the UK were, of course, prompted by UK interests rather than support and concern for Hong Kong. The talks continued into the night. Just after midnight, the USA laid it on the line. President Nixon was scheduled to make a statement at noon on the following day, in fact, later that day. The Hong Kong Delegation was shown two texts. The first announced that the USA and Hong Kong had reached agreement on the voluntary restraint by Hong Kong of its exports of garments and fabrics of man-made fibres and blends thereof, and wool. It went on to say how much the US valued the co-operation of the Hong Kong government and its recognition of the particular difficulties being experienced by the US textile industry. The second announced that the president had that morning at nine o'clock' signed an Executive Order under the authority of the Agriculture Act that banned all imports of man-made fibre and wool products from Hong Kong beyond the levels reached two years previously

'You chose which one you want', said the leader of the US side. It was not Hong Kong's finest hour. This was the way hardball politics were played. There was a flurry of telephone calls between the Hong Kong team in Washington and the Governor. London intervened to ask for an update. After another two hours of gruelling negotiations, Hong Kong finally capitulated.

I found myself locked up in the State Department at three o'clock in the morning drafting the agreement by hand in pencil on a rough pad. There were no typewriters or typists around at that hour. I was surrounded by the exhausted members of both teams snatching a few moments' sleep. The hand-written agreement was finally initialled at 3.45 a.m. and the president informed.

The negotiation was not without its lighter moments. When I was halfway through the drafting of the agreement, the direct line telephone that had been put through to the meeting room by the switchboard before everyone went home, rang. A very English voice said 'Hello, this is the FCO in London. Is there anybody there that knows anything about textiles?' Not many foreigners get to work the telephone in State Department at three o'clock in the morning. I answered as politely as I could in the circumstances.

'Oh, you do?' said the voice. 'I say, have you chaps really thought this textile thing through? You know we here in London believe it would be awfully awkward if you chaps caved in. Oh, you have? I see. All right, thank you very much. Good morning'. The further irony was that the voice was that of Ben Meynell, who would later be my adversary across the EEC negotiating table and pressing Hong Kong to restrain its exports of mmf textiles, among others.

We always stayed at the Watergate Hotel on our visits to Washington. It somehow seemed appropriate for we usually left robbed of our access rights by agents of the White House, only in our case, in the guise of the US negotiating team. On this occasion, Peter Tsao's room was really burgled. With the resourcefulness that was to mark him out for greater things to come, he successfully persuaded the Treasury on his return to Hong Kong that the thieves had stolen the delegation's imprest but left his own money untouched.

Chapter Seven
The Multi-Fibre Arrangement:
The Fifth Piece of Paper

By the beginning of 1973, international trade in textiles and garments was subject to a network of restrictions arising from the use of the LTA for cotton textiles, and voluntary export restraints for those of man-made fibres and blends thereof, and in some cases, wool. All those exercising restraint or volunteering so to do were developing countries, and all those applying restraints were developed countries. The one major exception was Japan. It had got rid of most of the restrictions that applied after the end of the Second World War but had had to accept restrictions on textiles (and some other products) as the price it had to pay. The LTA, originally intended to run for four years, had been extended in 1966 and again in 1970 for further four-year periods. With the prospect of yet another extension, it was clear that the LTA was no longer relevant. Restraints had moved beyond cotton. What is more, since the non-cotton restrictions were voluntary, there were no rules or parameters which governed their negotiation. It was unrealistic to expect that all restrictions would disappear once the twice-renewed LTA expired at the end of 1974. But if they were to continue, then it would be better to have some new rules to provide a framework for them. This should take account of experience with the LTA and the voluntary agreements, and establish a new basis for the negotiation and implementation of restrictions. At the same time, it should provide some protection from abuse by the developed countries by requiring real justification for any restraints requested. Negotiations for a new international instrument were held under the auspices of the GATT in Geneva throughout 1973.

By now, Hong Kong held the unenviable record of having the most restraints on its exports of textiles and garments for the longest period of time. As a consequence, it made quite sure that its voice was heard in Geneva, despite the fact that the United Kingdom supposedly had international responsibility for its dependent territory. The problem was that Hong Kong's interests and those of the UK were diametrically opposed. Bill Dorward, who was Acting Deputy Director of Commerce and Industry, was sent as Hong Kong's representative. Dorward quickly established a reputation for being a tough but reasonable negotiator. Some of the other developing countries, having suffered to some extent from Hong Kong's forced predominance in the field of restricted exports, and having noted how Hong Kong had conducted itself during the many negotiations it had undertaken since volunteering to help Lancashire some fifteen years previously, began to fall in with Hong Kong's line. An unofficial group of developing countries was set up and when matters concerning garments were discussed, Hong Kong was recognised as the *primus inter pares*. Nonetheless, suspicion about Hong Kong continued. There were still doubts as to how much (nothing!) passed between Hong Kong and the UK on negotiating positions, etc. After some tough multi-lateral negotiations and hard bargaining at the very end of December 1973, it was agreed that the hodge-podge of cotton restraint agreements, voluntary export restraints and import restrictions that were in operation would all be subsumed into the Arrangement Regarding International Trade in Textiles. The new Arrangement covered trade in textiles products of cotton, man-made fibres, wool and blends thereof and set out new rules for its governance. It was agreed that it would come into force on 1 January 1974 for a period of four years (Article 16).

Having delivered the new Arrangement, Dorward was sent to Geneva to become Hong Kong's representative to the GATT and nominee to the new Textiles Surveillance Body that had been set up. I moved up to Acting Deputy Director of Commerce and Industry charged with negotiating the new generation of textile agreements under the MFA and implementing the results.

The Arrangement Regarding International Trade in Textiles, commonly known as the Multi-Fibre Arrangement or MFA, was the fifth piece of paper of importance for Hong Kong and by far the most significant. It was an extraordinary instrument for several reasons.

Firstly, it failed completely to achieve its intended purpose but stood as the most enduring of temporary trade measures, lasting for over thirty years. Secondly, it acted as a safety-valve for avoiding the restrictive use of Article XIX of the GATT and the complications that would have arisen therefrom. Thirdly, it created the intriguing paradox encapsulated in the title of this book: Hong Kong emerged as the world's number one exporter of garments and the world's thirteenth largest exporter overall, prospering while upholding its free trade principles through the acceptance of increasing restrictions on its most important industry, its largest export earner and its biggest employer of labour. It could even be argued that the only textile industry ever protected by the MFA was that of Hong Kong as it established the territory as the dominant supplier in a restricted market. Fourthly, its ramifications persist in Hong Kong to this day to the extent that the income derived from the export of textiles and garments provided the capital for its further development as a manufacturing, commercial and financial centre. Finally, the MFA disappeared without a murmur in 2005 and no one seems any the worse for its passing.

But, to be fair, at the start, the MFA was seen as a new and sensible way to deal realistically with the political and economic pressures prevalent in the developed countries. With the EEC's common commercial policy yet to be finalised, Italy entered the MFA with great enthusiasm. Much to the consternation of the USA and the amusement of the other participating countries, it had assumed the MFA meant what it said. It, therefore, claimed that fabric imports from the USA were causing disruption in the Italian market. Italy was gently led to one side and had the facts of life explained. Their request for consultations disappeared from the records and was never heard of again.

Some brief outline of the content of the MFA is necessary for an understanding of the line Hong Kong took in its negotiations as well as the way in which it implemented the results. Article 1 expressed worthy sentiments about the need to achieve the expansion and liberalisation of trade, reduce barriers to trade, and further the economic and social development of developing countries. Then comes the 'however'. Special measures of international co-operation 'may be desirable' during the following few years to eliminate difficulties in the field of textiles. The Article also states that damage should be avoided to the 'minimum viable production' (MVP) of countries having small markets, a high level of imports and a low level of domestic production. The Nordic countries insisted on the insertion of this clause claiming it represented their circumstances. It became known as the Nordic or MVP clause. What it actually meant was never made clear. Article 2 required that all existing agreements on textiles and garments be brought into line with the MFA and all illegal restrictions removed. For Hong Kong, this meant France (at last) and Japan. Article 3 was a key article. This prohibits any new restrictions on textiles unless they are causing 'market disruption', as defined in Annex A of the MFA. Such restrictions had to be limited to the precise products that were causing market disruption and justified by a 'detailed factual statement of the reasons and justification for the request' for restraint. This was similar in intent to Article 3 of the previous LTA but emphasised the need for proper justification for the restrictions. Article 4 was the other key article. This too was similar to the LTA's Article 4 and allowed mutually acceptable arrangements between two 'participating countries' provided they were consistent 'with the basic objectives and principles' of the MFA, and, more importantly 'on overall terms, including base levels and growth rates' were more liberal than the measures provided for in Article 3. Article 8 asked participating countries to take steps to avoid circumvention of the MFA by 'trans-shipment, re-routing or action by non-participants'. Article 10 established a Textiles Committee under the auspices of the GATT consisting of representatives of all the participating countries. Ominously, one of the duties of the new Committee was to meet no later than one year before the expiry of the MFA in order to consider whether it should be 'extended, modified, or discontinued'. Article 11 established a Textiles Surveillance Body (TSB). The TSB was charged with overseeing the operation of the MFA and considering any disputes between the participating countries. Article 12 defined the products covered by the MFA in terms of the weight or value of the component fibres. It specifically excluded 'traditional folklore handicraft textiles products and artificial and synthetic staple fibre, tow, waste, and simple mono- and multi-filaments', none of which were of interest to Hong Kong.

Annex A defined market disruption and the factors said to cause it. Annex B was very important for it contained a number of rules affecting the application of the MFA:

- roll-back period: the minimum level below which exports could not be restrained;
- growth factor: where restrictions continued for a year or more, the restraint level had to be increased by not less than 6 percent each year; a lower but positive amount could be agreed;
- swing factor: where restraint was applied to more than one product, the limit for that product could be exceeded by 7 percent provided the aggregate limit for all restrained products was not exceeded; another percentage could be agreed but not less than 5 percent;
- carry forward: an amount up to 5 percent could be borrowed from the following year's limits;
- carryover: any unused amount remaining at the end of a restraint period could be carried over into the immediately following year up to a

maximum of 10 percent less any amount taken under the carry forward provision.

These then the basic rules which were to apply. Perhaps the most significant advance made in the MFA was the creation of the Textiles Surveillance Body (TSB) to oversee the operation of the MFA and examine the content of all restraint agreements for conformity with its provisions. Permanent seats were held by the USA, the EEC and Japan. The Nordic countries shared another seat while Hong Kong shared one with South Korea. Egypt, Pakistan, and India were also represented as were the countries of South America.

Since no one wanted to remove restrictions on Hong Kong textiles while some hoped to add more, all Hong Kong's agreements with other countries had to be renegotiated to bring them into line with the new MFA. Fortunately, none of the agreements then in force expired before the end of 1974. DC&I had taken this step in anticipation of a new international arrangement of some sort and to ensure a minimum of disruption to the trade while new negotiations were being held. The EEC was making progress towards the adoption of a common commercial policy so the renegotiation of Hong Kong's agreement with the six original members of the EEC would have to be with the expanded Community of nine Member States. This now included the United Kingdom, Denmark and Ireland, and meant that the agreements then in force with the UK and Denmark would have to be subsumed in a new EEC/Hong Kong agreement. The renegotiation of all the restraint agreements, covering a textile and garment trade now worth in excess of thirty billion dollars was a daunting task. I was the new boy, at the sharp end, with a brand-new agreement that had yet to be tested. Inevitably, Hong Kong would be the first to use it, and everyone would be watching to see how it worked out.

I was very fortunate in five respects. First, I had moved up through the various sections, branches and divisions of the department over the preceding fifteen years, and had a reasonable knowledge of the 'nuts and bolts' aspects of trade officering. Secondly, and more importantly, while working in these various posts in DC&I, I had been a member of many if not most of Hong Kong's negotiating teams over the years and learned much from my predecessors as Chief Trade Negotiator. These included such luminaries as Sir John Cowperthwaite himself, Ronnie Holmes, Philip Haddon-Cave, David Jordan, Eric Ho and Bill Dorward. Thirdly, by 1974, the majority of the middle management and senior posts within the DC&I were filled by Trade Officers, who, like me, had grown up with the department and provided a sound back-up and support system for our negotiations. Without in any way taking anything from the abilities of my other colleagues in the Trade Officer Grade, four officers were of outstanding ability and stood out as automatic choices for the negotiating teams. These were Peter Tsao, who had no equal in finding ingenious ways of getting out of seemingly impossible situations, Justin Yue, a shrewd tactician with organisational skills that were to earn him an MBE and T. H. 'Brian' Chau, who did not suffer fools gladly (although we got on well together) and whose fiery and incisive demolition of the pious platitudes of the developed countries in international meetings was eagerly awaited by the developing countries. On at least one occasion, the Director General of the GATT intervened to say he was about to call in the Fire Brigade. Finally, there was Michael Wu, a whizz-kid with numbers who could assemble statistics in ways that could prove one thing or its direct opposite as the occasion required. All four, later in their careers, went on to bigger things. On top of this, we had a first class Director in David Jordan, who defended his department and its role against all comers. Although an Administrative Officer, he received the ultimate accolade from the Trade Officer Grade — they made him an honorary Trade Officer on his retirement. The fourth advantage was to have the TEXTAB to advise both on tactics and the technical implications for the Hong Kong industry and trade of any particular restraint. The final advantage was that our very first MFA negotiation – the MFA was barely a month old - was with the Austrians, who had always conducted themselves impeccably in our previous negotiations. The Austrian team was led by Dr Gotfried Dinzl, a real gentleman from the old school. He insisted to his own industry advisors that they should follow the MFA to the letter, then, asked us if we would mind explaining what the various articles meant. Thereafter we had exploratory talks or negotiations with the USA, the UK, Sweden, Norway, Canada, Australia and Japan. 1974 seemed to pass very quickly.

The most significant of these was our first negotiation with the USA under the MFA in May 1974. Both sides were on their best behaviour recognising the importance of preserving the sanctity of the new international instrument. We began talks with the US side on Monday and by Thursday evening had an agreement. Everyone was amazed. Both sides earned the plaudits of their constituencies. I worried that I had missed a trick or done something wrong. The big name missing from this list was the EEC. We had had problems enough with the Community in negotiating an agreement under the previous Long

Term Arrangement. Before the common commercial policy was finalised, individual member states were allowed to negotiate directly with Hong Kong. Italy requested consultations with Hong Kong on men's cotton handkerchiefs. A portly but extremely pleasant gentleman holding a thick brown dossier walked into the Conference Room in Fire Brigade Building, said 'buon giorno', tripped on the carpet and spilled his papers all over the floor. He re-assembled them with some difficulty but considerable dignity, said he would need to go back to Rome for further instructions and departed the next day. The Hong Kong Government thoughtfully provided a car to take him to the airport. France requested consultations on ladies' underwear. Senior French and Hong Kong civil servants solemnly retired to the Quai d'Orsay to consider the disruption caused by French knickers, made in Hong Kong. A significant problem emerged over 'slips'. The Hong Kong export figures and French import statistics were miles apart. Despite their best efforts, and recounts in Hong Kong and Paris, the two sides could get no nearer to explaining the wide discrepancy. At this stage, the French side produced some samples and gravely passed them round the room for inspection. The problem then became clear. By 'slips', the Hong Kong side, steeped in years of colonial rule, had understood the term to mean a petticoat ('Your slip is showing, my dear'). In French, on the other hand, 'les slips' meant a type of ladies' panties. How could mere civil servants be expected to know such things? Once the two sides understood these mysteries of a lady's nether-world, they quickly reached a mutually amicable settlement.

I recall a tense meeting in Stockholm when Sweden tried to persuade us that our exports of woollen sweaters were disrupting their market and injuring domestic producers. We listened patiently to the usual arguments about 'fair trade' and 'level playing fields' and 'sweatshops' as well as lectures about low prices arising from the terrible working conditions in Hong Kong. As I have mentioned elsewhere, we prepared meticulously for any negotiation, however large or small. By the time it came to my turn to reply, the team had studied our trade analysis sheet and highlighted key passages in yellow. I was able to point out that Hong Kong represented only the third largest supplier to the Swedish market and was not the cheapest. Swedish industry itself was the largest supplier selling at roughly the same price as Hong Kong on a like for like basis. Swedish manufacturers were closely followed by Portugal whose exports were considerably higher than Hong Kong's and prices lower.

'This is because Portugal is our EFTA partner and we have a legal obligation to accept them', responded the leader of the Swedish side, as if this offered full justification for his position and total demolition of mine. He seemed unaware of the contractual obligations he had with Hong Kong under the GATT and the MFA. Nor was he amused when I wondered aloud whether Hong Kong, as a real free trade area, might join their Free Trade Area.

I went on to point out that our research had revealed that a significant number of the Portuguese factories supplying sweaters to Sweden were in fact owned and operated by Swedish companies. I presumed that this was to take advantage of lower standards applying in Portugal than in Sweden, the same charge that was being made against Hong Kong. I finished by saying that the only conclusion that could be drawn from the facts was that, if (emphasised) the Swedish market was being disrupted and its industry damaged by imports, then, it must be due to Swedish manufacturers disrupting their own market and injuring themselves. The Swedish government was, therefore, talking to the wrong people if it thought Hong Kong was to blame. That particular negotiation ended with Hong Kong agreeing to restrain its exports on a narrower range of goods at increased quantities; after all, we did not want to disrupt exports of the Hong Kong sweater industry on a mere point of principle.

The negotiation with the EEC as a whole always threatened to be a tough one. The delay in coming to the negotiating table was due to the EEC's need to have a common commercial policy on textiles that was acceptable to nine different member states, each with a view on how to deal with imports from Hong Kong. We did not get to meet the EEC until 1975. By this time we had more or less perfected the way we made our preparations for trade negotiations and the way we conducted ourselves in the meeting-room. Our first task involved drawing up our negotiating brief. We would prepare a consultative paper outlining the background to the negotiation, the realistic possibilities of what we might be able to achieve, our 'brick wall' — the point beyond which the negotiating team would not go without seeking further instructions, and a recommendation as to how to proceed. This would first be considered by the Textiles Advisory Board. For a major negotiation, such as the renegotiation of the MFA itself, we would present a paper incorporating the views of TEXTAB to the Executive Council, a reflection of the importance of textiles for the Hong Kong economy. The Governor always kept a watchful eye on the progress of negotiations and stood available as a weapon of last resort if EEC demands became too outrageous. The Board gave invaluable advice: where to soft-pedal, where to press for the best we could get and where to reluctantly concede so we would have 'swing' yardage. On their advice (and that of EXCO, when consulted), we would prepare to do battle.

As mentioned earlier, one of the requirements of the MFA was that the demandeurs should provide a 'detailed factual statement of the reasons and justification for the request' for restraint. The first few offerings we received were sparsely detailed, rarely factual, and usually without justification. When it became clear that we did our homework anyway, countries took much more care with their own preparations since, so often, we caught them out with their own figures obtained from various sources. Our key document consisted of a single sheet of A4 paper on which we assembled a mass of statistical data. With regard to each product under discussion, we could tell at a glance a country's total imports of the product, the five principal sources of imports, the value of imports, retained imports (imports minus exports), domestic production, domestic producers' share of their market, Hong Kong's share of imports and the whole market, the market share of other suppliers and so on. We could usually give the other side a run for their money when it came to talking about numbers. Once we had our briefing instructions from the Board, we would appoint the negotiating team, automatically selecting Messrs. Tsao, Yue, Chau and Wu, if available. If we travelled overseas, we also took the desk-officer responsible for the area or subject under discussion, an Assistant Trade Officer, for the experience and as note-taker and general factotum and a personal secretary. If we went to London, Geneva, Washington or Brussels, the DC&I man in these cities joined the team. For major negotiations, the entire TEXTAB accompanied us; for lesser ones, at least two members of the Board came. We also took someone from Legal Department if there was a likelihood of a lot of legal drafting to be done. All of which may seem extravagant until compared with the resources available to those with whom we were negotiating: and we were several thousand miles from home base. We stayed in a hotel convenient to the venue where the negotiations were held. I had a suite, which sounds grand but wasn't. It was used as the team office, for private discussions with the leaders of the other side, as the meeting-room for TEXTAB, for press briefings with journalists, as a communal restaurant until the Chinese members could take no more Western food and insisted on visiting the local Chinese eateries and for vicious games of Scrabble or Battleships, when we had enforced waits while the other side consulted with its constituents. I was allowed to travel first class by air. This privilege was available only to the top five or six posts in government: it was extended to the Chief Trade Negotiator because of the frequency and distances that had to be travelled in getting from Hong Kong to our main customers overseas. It was a privilege that had been secured in typical fashion by David Jordan when he served as Chief Trade Negotiator. Tucked away in Government Regulations were some obscure rules that said if making an air journey longer than five hours, an officer was entitled to take two days acclimatisation leave on arrival at destination and another two days on return. This was before long-haul, non-stop, flights had been invented. Another regulation said that all flights to Europe should be by British (Overseas) Airways.

On one occasion, no sooner had David arrived back from a gruelling trip across the Pacific than he had to fly off to Brussels. He was not amused when the Treasury informed him proudly that, with much difficulty, at such short-notice, it had managed to find him an economy seat on BOAC to London. David's eloquent response pointed out, in somewhat forceful terms that the loss of four days work of a senior government officer, which his work would not allow him to do anyway, and the cost of two additional days in an hotel more than compensated for the cost of a first-class ticket. When the Secretariat rejected this view, David wrote directly to the Governor to the effect that 'I have just returned from Washington. I need to go to Brussels. Someone has booked me to go to London instead. If I am to go, I insist on travelling first class to my desired destination. If I am not to travel in this way, I am happy to pass the job to someone else'. And that was how he and subsequent Chief Trade Negotiators got to travel first class.

Peter Tsao secured another perquisite as regards accounting for our stay overseas as a consequence of his personal Watergate moment. The Treasury was very hot on controlling the spending of public funds by public servants. The policy seemed to be that the less the significance of the expenditure, the more strict the rules. Type of hotel, nature of expense, class of travel, and the like were all subject to draconian regulation, while the absence of a receipt was viewed as bordering on embezzlement. One Trade Officer who had been on a trade mission to Egypt was asked for a translation of his Arabic bus ticket. After the theft of the imprest and the delegation's records in Washington, the Treasury had a rethink. I am not sure whether it applied to everybody, but from then on, if a trade negotiation had an approved budget, we consolidated our bills for room, food, laundry, taxis, and so on and the Treasury paid up. This saved an enormous amount of time and effort.

In the conference room itself, we had strict rules of conduct. On the first day, the Chief Trade Negotiator introduced his team and explained the duties of each member. Thereafter, he was the only person who spoke for Hong Kong unless he invited one of his team to respond on a particular point. If in the view of a team member, the leader was moving off-message or going in the wrong direction, the team member would write a brief note and pass it to the leader. Depending on the content of the note, the leader would change tack, or ask for a short break to discuss the point in whispers (or Cantonese) with the team. If a major issue arose, the leader would ask for a recess and the whole subject would be reviewed, with the TEXTAB if necessary.

Outside the formal meetings, things were different. Many of the exchanges within the meeting-room were for the record and for the benefit of any constituents who might be present. This was particularly the case in discussions with the EEC. Under internal Community arrangements the practice was that the European Commission spoke on behalf of the member states after they had reached a common position on the product or provision under discussion. Because nine Members had to agree, it was virtually impossible for any EEC negotiator to show any flexibility in his position across the negotiating table with nine member states breathing down his neck. It was therefore outside the meeting-room, and, usually in my suite, that the real negotiation took place between the Hong Kong team and a few selected Commission officials. These talks were off the record and a general free-for-all. It was much the same with other countries. In the USA, Labour and Commerce Departments were the hawks; State Department and the White House staff less so.

In the evening, we briefed the TEXTAB on what had happened during the day. These were always full briefings: we worked on the principle that if you appointed people to give you advice, there was not much point in then concealing unpalatable aspects of the day's play from them.

When that was done we dictated a detailed record of the day's proceedings and TEXTAB's reaction to it to the personal secretary, who, poor lady, had to get it right first time, type it up and send it via the hotel's fax machine so that it arrived on Hong Kong desks by nine o'clock the following morning. We used a secretary from Hong Kong because they knew the subject matter, were highly accurate and accustomed to working all hours of the day and night.

In the early days of our trade negotiations overseas, we were under instructions to send back situation reports in the form of cipher-telegrams to Hong Kong each day. This meant that the text had first to be taken to the nearest British Embassy. There, the Coding Officer, usually late at night, had to encipher and despatch the telegram with copies to the Foreign and Commonwealth

Office in London, and British Embassies in Washington, Brussels and Geneva. Telegrams were also copied to the British Consul in Tamsui in Taiwan, who kept begging to be left off the mailing list since he had to do the decoding himself, and knew nothing about textiles or Taiwan's position on the subject anyway. It also meant that someone in the Hong Kong team had to spend the night ensuring everything got away, and was thus useless for any work the following day. At the receiving ends, the telegrams had to be decoded and circulated who knew where. The Hong Kong teams were not at all keen on the idea that their reports, intended for the Hong Kong government and its overseas Councuillors, might be seen by all and sundry in the FCO and UK posts overseas. Nor was Hong Kong absolutely certain that telegram traffic was not being intercepted by some of the countries about whom Hong Kong might be making rude remarks. Once the security man in the Hong Kong Government who had required all these things to be done was moved to another job, as I have said, all reports were sent every night, plain language, using the hotel's fax machine: much more secure and much more difficult for anyone to intercept. The fax message also went straight into the hands of Hong Kong's own Counsellors without being seen by other friendly eyes.

In Hong Kong government archives there should be a daily record of every trade negotiation during the period, which would be a gold mine for any dedicated researcher with the time and inclination.

After we had got our report off to Hong Kong, we went to bed, got up the next morning, and did the same thing all over again.

Once agreement had been reached with a country, we returned to Hong Kong and began the equally challenging task of converting what was on paper into real trade opportunities for our exporters and manufacturers.

Part Two

The Emerging Paradox and Some Other Diversions

Chapter Eight
Making It Work

Hong Kong enjoyed its greatest success with the implementation of its restraint agreements and maximising the opportunities within them.

The entire control system was built and operated based on the advice of the Textiles Advisory Board, whose wise words earned the grateful thanks of the industry they represented and much criticism from outsiders.

The key document to the whole of the export control system was the textile export licence (E/L). No ship could load a textiles consignment without one. The ship's manifest was checked against a copy of the E/L held by the DC&1. The E/L contained the name of the ship, and the date on which it sailed, and all the information needed to identify the product covered by the licence, the category of the product, the quantity, and the country to which it was being shipped. It incorporated legal declarations by manufacturer and exporter as to the veracity of the information contained within it. False declarations were pursued in the Courts with severe penalties for offenders.

Since the E/L was required for all shipments of textiles, the E/L served as a detailed factual record of every textile product that left Hong Kong for every market in the world. When a request for restraint arose therefore, Hong Kong was able to give precise details of its exports down to the last piece right up to the previous day. Importing countries often found this very disconcerting when trying to match their (much-delayed) import statistics with Hong Kong's export data.

The reader will have noticed the emphasis throughout this history that has been placed on exports and export controls. This is more than a question of choice of words. Export control was a sine qua non for every one of Hong Kong's restraint agreements from the very first to the very last. Export control gives commercial advantage. If orders and quotas were in the hands of importers, they would be able to hawk their orders around and force down prices while exporters and manufacturers competed to secure a share of a limited supply of quota. With quotas in the hands of exporters, however, the buyer has to compete for quotas held by those at the export end who will charge prices to the full extent the market will bear. Such commercial advantage is small compared to the loss of business inherent in any restraint on trade.

The only time the TEXTAB got nervous was when a country threatened unilateral import controls. Although such controls would almost certainly be illegal under the GATT, politics could always override such niceties. It was this threat of import controls that had persuaded Hong Kong to volunteer controls on exports of man-made fibres to the USA during the Nixon era. Eventually, when Hong Kong was the predominant supplier with the most restraints, it devised a contingency plan for dealing with imposed import controls. Fortunately, this was never needed and remains under wraps to this day—just in case.

The control system comprised a number of phases. The actual conduct of a negotiation leading to a restraint agreement is covered elsewhere in this story but once agreement had been reached, the Q (=quota) Division of DC&I swung into action. Its first task was to establish who had shipped how many of what during a given reference time-frame, usually but not always the 'roll-back period' of Annex B of the MFA. This information was collated from the copies of export licences held by the department. The total amount shipped as recorded by the E/Ls was then compared with the restraint limit set out in the Agreement. Where the Agreement limit was lower than the actual previous trade level, as was usually the case, past performance was scaled back on a proportionate basis. Where the restraint limit was higher, any excess was set aside for later use.

Each company's performance during the reference period was then calculated and reduced proportionately if necessary. 'Company' meant the manufacturer and the exporter of the goods. Amounts were calculated on the basis of 50 percent of the proportionate amount available to the exporter and 50 percent to the manufacturer. Once this fifty/fifty split became standard practice, many manufacturers established their own export departments. By so doing, they qualified for 100 percent of the amount available, although nominally this was by reference to the fifty/fifty split.

Quotas were always offered to qualifying companies before they were allocated. This was because they were subject to certain conditions. If these were accepted, the quota was then allocated.

The conditions were that the company undertook to obtain an export licence for at least 95 percent of the amount offered within eleven months. Since most agreements ran for a number of years in twelve month periods, a company would receive, in the following 'quota' year, an offer of another 100 percent plus a proportion of any growth factor that was incorporated in the Agreement for the following year. Any company that exported less than 95 percent but more than 50 percent of the amount offered, would in a following year, be offered a further allocation equal to the percentage utilised in the previous year. Any company that exported 50 percent or less of the amount offered would not be entitled to any further allocation.

There was thus a considerable incentive for a company to use its quotas fully if it was to stay in business. It also meant that quota hoarding to try to force prices up was a very risky business since a failure to ship 95 percent or more meant a loss both of quota and a share of the growth factor for the following year.

Once the company accepted these terms, a quota account was opened for the company which was then free to apply for an export licence for that product up to the total of its quota allocation at any time within the first eleven months of the quota year.

The eleven-month requirement operated as another device to ensure that quotas were fully used. Once the twelve-month period had expired, no further shipments against that year's quotas could be made (unless carry over arrangements had been previously agreed with the importing country). The E/L was valid for 30 days except for the last month of the year when its validity decreased in keeping with the amount of the year that was left. So a shipment to be made in the last month could be licensed at the end of the eleventh month. As a consequence, by the end of the eleventh month, it was possible to calculate how much of Hong Kong's quotas had been committed for shipment before the end of the year and how much remained unutilised. Special arrangements were then made to use up any amounts outstanding. These are described later.

The quota holding was something akin to a bank balance, except that the initial deposit was given by DC&I in proportion to a company's past performance as exporter or manufacturer. The quota holder then had to run the account down to zero in twelve months, and, if this was done, another deposit, perhaps slightly larger than the first, was made to the quota holder's account.

This was a simple enough system for the company. Behind the scenes it involved a considerable amount of work for the DC&I, a large number of staff, and a great deal of accuracy.

Under the MFA, Hong Kong had restraint arrangements at various times with eighteen countries: Austria, Australia, the three Benelux countries, Canada, Denmark, Finland, France, Germany, Greece, Ireland, Italy, Norway, Portugal, Spain, Sweden, Switzerland, the United Kingdom and the United States of America.

Each of these countries had different requirements as to product coverage, different definitions of products, different restraint limits, different time periods and different structures for their Agreements. For each country, there were thousands of Hong Kong manufacturers and exporters, each with different past performances as the basis for the allocation of quotas. Such quotas had to be individually calculated and controlled on a company by country by product by quantity basis. Each single piece exported had to be properly accounted for and licensed. Any errors, unintentional or deliberate, would have been pounced upon by the importing country, always ready to find a reason to cut back Hong Kong. On top of all of this, the swing, carryover and carry forward provisions of an Agreement had to be exploited to the full to provide the Hong Kong company with the greatest possible flexibility in responding to market needs, and required further calculations for each quota holding.

Following one negotiation with the EEC, the whole of the categorisation system was changed. This involved the recalculation and redistribution of quotas for every company with past performance in any category of goods for each of the nine Member States. It coincided with a particularly heavy buying season, when it was essential that companies should know exactly how much quota they would have for the coming year. The job was given to Justin Yue. We closed early on Friday afternoon, drafted in over a hundred volunteer clerks from other government departments, trained them for an hour on how to calculate quotas, commandeered as many abacuses and calculating machines as we needed and worked in shifts round the clock. By nine o'clock Monday morning, quota allocation letters were available for collection by individual companies from the department. And there was a queue waiting for them. For this mammoth task, Justin Yue was awarded the MBE in the Queen's Honours.

Today, it is likely that all of this could be done by computers at the touch of a button. In the late 1950s and 1960s, the only buttons used were those on the abacus. All shipments were calculated by hand, laboriously entered in great ledgers and balanced at the end of each day. It was not until the early 1970s that the DC&I ventured into computerisation. Computers at that time could not meet the full system's needs, however, and only a simple accounting programme — quantity in, quantity out, was introduced. This eased the work-load a bit, but once anything beyond that was required, it had to be done by hand.

There must have been several hundred thousand individual quota holdings in total. No one ever found time to count exactly how many.

The procedure followed was that the exporter/manufacturer made an application for an export licence in triplicate for the country, product, and quantity he wanted to ship, two working days before shipment. The application was matched with the company's account to check he had sufficient quota for that product to that market. The quantity to be exported was then deducted from the company's quota holding and two copies of the application were handed back to the company suitably endorsed by the DC&I. These copies then became the export licence. The company kept one copy for its records and took the other E/L with the cargo to the ship where it was checked by the ship for accuracy. The cargo was then loaded and entered on the ship's manifest. A copy of the manifest accompanied by the relevant surrendered export licences were returned to the DC&I in due course where they were checked for accuracy against the copy licence held by the Department. Because of the nature of the trade and production runs, manufacturers were allowed to revise the amount shown on the E/L downwards provided it was initialled by the company and the ship's captain. No one was allowed to revise the quantity upwards. Where such changes were made, the E/L was referred back to the quota accounts section and the unshipped amount was credited back to the quota holder. The fact that such fine adjustments were made was a reflection of the importance and value of quota to the quota holder and the determination of the DC&I to adhere scrupulously to the restraint limits while using them down to the last piece.

The carryover and carry forward provisions of an agreement were useful to have but not often taken advantage of. The way the control system operated meant that there was rarely anything left to carry over. Companies were reluctant to use carry forward, borrowing from the following year, because it meant they would have less quota in the following year while if they took increased amounts in the current year, greater supply might reduce prices. Again when to use and when not was a matter for the TEXTAB to determine and advise.

The swing provisions, however, were particularly advantageous and always used in full. They provided that a quantity of one product could be used to ship a quantity of some other product using an agreed square yards or square metres (yet another accounting complication!) conversion factor.

The swing schemes were operated in three phases throughout the year. In Phase One, usually implemented in the early part of the quota year, all companies were allowed to increase any holding they had in any category by the swing factor in the Agreement, say 5 percent, provided an equivalent amount was surrendered from some other category. Adjustments were then made to individual quota holdings. Clearly, this had no bearing on Hong Kong's overall limits since swings were paid off by roundabouts. In Phase Two of the scheme, halfway through the year, the DC&I calculated the quantitative amounts by which each individual category could be increased. This information was available once each company had made its own dispositions. The quantitative information was disseminated to the trade through a Notice to Exporters and applications for the available amounts accompanied by equivalent surrenders were invited. Where a particular category was over-subscribed, allocations were made on a proportionate basis. In this way, an individual company might be able to increase its own swing margin beyond the percentage recorded in the Agreement in quantitative terms without Hong Kong exceeding the restraint limit in overall terms. Towards the end of the quota year, a Phase Three, similar to Phase Two was introduced to provide a final opportunity to maximise this valuable flexibility provision.

Since all swing 'in' had to be accompanied by an equivalent swing 'out', companies had to make a fine choice between which category to increase and which to decrease. Based on the advice of the TEXTAB, Hong Kong was sometimes reluctantly persuaded by the importing country to accept restraint on a not very popular category. This then became the feeder category from which 'swing out' yardage was derived. Swinging out from piece-goods into garments was a particular favourite until importing countries rumbled what was going on.

The last move to ensure full utilisation of quotas was the Year End Special Shipment Scheme (YESSS). Under this scheme, all uncommitted amounts of quota were calculated. These could be derived from those companies that had not licensed 95 percent or more of their quotas in the year, or any excess of restraint limit over 'past performance' and amounts uncommitted after the first eleven months of the year. These were offered to all-comers on a first-come-first-served basis against production of a firm buyer's order. Any shipment under the YESSS qualified as past performance in calculating the following year's allocations.

So much for textile trade subject to restrictions. What about Hong Kong's textile trade that was yet to be the target of demands for restraint by importunate industries and their politically motivated governments, anxious to please them?

The imposition of restraints is extremely disruptive to all parties to the trade. Buyers find they cannot take delivery of their orders and exporters have nothing to export. Stuck between the two could be goods already in transit but suddenly with nowhere to go. Manufacturers could be in the middle of a production run only to find the intended recipient of their goods could no longer accept them.

Initially, requests to halt exports and enter into restraint negotiations caused serious problems for the DC&I and the trade. They complicated negotiations in determining how to deal with work in progress and goods in transit. A further problem was the 'roll-back' formula of MFA Annex B, which required that products be restrained to the twelve-month level of trade reached three months prior to the call for restraint.

Hong Kong then came up with the idea of the Export Authorisation (E/A) system. Whether it was a TEXTAB suggestion or dreamed up by a bright civil servant is now lost in the annals of time. Whoever it was deserves a pat on the back and the grateful thanks of all those involved. At one go, it solved the problem of chaotic disruption to the trade, allowed a breathing space for exports to continue, pending the finalisation of negotiations and became a useful negotiating tool.

The essence of the E/A system was that it conferred on its holder a guarantee that any goods covered by an E/A would be granted an export licence, and could be shipped to, and would be accepted by, the intended destination.

The first essential of the E/A system was that the importing country was prepared to accept it. Most countries were happy to do so because of the benefits both sides derived from it.

The system was available in respect of all unrestrained products or as many unrestrained categories as the importing country might nominate.

Any company in Hong Kong (including 'newcomers') with a firm order from a buyer in the importing country could apply for an E/A. It was issued with a three- or six-month validity period depending on the arrangements agreed with the importing country. It served as a temporary quota account, and, once issued, the company could apply for an export licence for any quantity up to the amount of the total order covered by the E/A. The company thus had a firm guarantee that the goods covered by it could be exported, and the importing country would accept the shipment. In essence, the E/A was a licence to get a licence.

A weekly (sometimes daily) report on the number of E/As issued for which products was forwarded to the authorities in the importing country who then had a three- or six-month forecast of the type of goods it would be receiving over the time period and in what quantities.

Some critics argued that this was playing into the hands of the importing countries and encouraging restrictions. Those in the business knew that it gave them security and minimised disruption to the trade if a call for restraint was made.

The E/A also became a useful negotiating tool. For example, once Hong Kong had agreed a 'comprehensive' Agreement with the USA, subsequent Agreements were also comprehensive. In other words, all exports of cotton, mmf and wool fabrics and apparel (to use the US terminology) were subject to limits of varying degrees of severity, depending on the quantity and 'sensitivity' of the item (code word for political pull of those making like products in the US). However, by the time the total equivalent square yardage of restraint limits on Hong Kong had reached one billion square yards, the US team felt that presentationally this would be unacceptable to the their textiles and garments lobbies. They would press for cut-backs (as the EEC was doing) and a host of new problems would be created. Neither side wanted that.

Hong Kong proposed that the 'comprehensive' Agreement be presented differently. One part would have an overall limit of equivalent square yards and cover those categories where there was said to be real concern. The other part would comprise all other categories with no overall ceiling or category limits but controlled under the Export Authorisation system. In this way, the billion square yards number would be reduced to about 700 million square yards, while the rest of the goods would be monitored daily under the E/A system and provide a detailed picture of what would be arriving at US ports on a rolling three-month basis.

The USA accepted this idea and both sides came out smelling of roses. The US team claimed that it had the major categories under tight restraint at a lower overall square yardage level while the E/A system on all other categories would allow the USA to call Hong Kong for consultations at any time on the basis of forecast shipments. Hong Kong, for its part, could claim that it was no worse off as regards the major categories — cut-backs had been avoided, and a considerable amount of trade had been 'freed' from restriction. It was the classic case of each side delivering what its constituents wanted to hear. Furthermore, importing countries, especially the EEC, were pressing for even tougher restraints and could see that the US precedent in no way favoured their efforts to increase the number of restrictions and reduce the quantities of goods, and that a similar solution for them would not be acceptable to their industries. (Of course, Hong Kong ran the risk of being 'called for consultations' at levels below those previously achieved but this was seen as acceptable given the dangers on the European horizon.) Other developing countries tried a similar ploy with the US but were less successful largely because they did not have the same effective export control systems and consequently did not have Hong Kong's reputation for scrupulously discharging its obligations. At US insistence, the HK/US Textile Agreement contained a reference to the uniqueness of the Hong Kong E/A Scheme and its effectiveness so that the USA did not have to offer a similar system to other restraining countries.

Interfering with trade has some remarkable consequences as Hong Kong and others were to discover.

One thing a businessman really values is certainty. That was one reason why the Export Authorisation System was such a success: companies knew they could get their orders away once covered by an E/A. Another 'certainty' was that if a category was brought under restraint, quotas would be issued by reference to past performance on a fifty/fifty basis, that the quota would continue in subsequent years provided it was fully used, and that quotas could be transferred, usually at a price, to facilitate the marriage of quota and order. Given this 'certainty', the DC&I was asked by local banks to say whether quota holdings could be considered assets of a company and taken into account when considering loan risk.

The DC&I's formal reply could only be that Hong Kong opposed restraints on trade in principle and its efforts were always directed to the removal of restrictions. Restraints on trade were only accepted where the alternative was something worse. Furthermore, it was impossible to say what line any particular importing country might take on any particular product at any particular time. What might have been seen as an asset on one day could have disappeared completely the next. The DC&I, therefore, could only conclude that quota holdings should not be considered as assets.

Fortunately for the economy, neither the banks nor the industry swallowed this line of argument. They were firmly of the view that at least short-term quotas were as good as, and, in some cases, better than money. Any textile company going 'public' on the Stock Exchange at this time made considerable play of its quota holdings in its prospectus. Any with significant holdings were usually subscribed several times over.

Another area affected by the textiles restraints was the shipping industry. Hong Kong by now was the world's largest exporter of garments, and the shipping lines went out of their way, literally, to obtain a slice of the action.

Every restraint agreement had a cut off date. At 23:59 hours on the last day of the quota year, any quota unshipped was 'lost'. The DC&I defined as 'unshipped' any product that had not been licensed for export or was not on board a ship that had cleared Waglan Lighthouse, harbour limits, by midnight. The Marine Department kept records of all such shipping movements and passed these to the DC&I for checking. For much of the year, ships were quite lax about when they sailed, and often hung around until holds were full. On the last day of the quota year, however, there was always a last-minute rush and ships of all kinds came to Hong Kong to help get cargo away.

They well knew that if they did not leave in good time, their customers' quota holdings would suffer. Many shipping lines sold space with an absolute guarantee that provided cargoes were delivered dock-side by a given time, the vessel would clear Waglan Lighthouse before midnight. There was a mass exodus of ships as they raced to beat the deadline.

The shipping lines squeezed every last drop from a restraint agreement as well. Ships with spare hold space would load the last of the current year's quota, and sail past Waglan Lighthouse just in time to meet the deadline. They then steamed round Hong Kong Island and returned to the harbour again through the Lei Yue Mun entrance in the first minutes of the new quota year, tied up alongside, and began loading cargo once more, this time, the first shipments against the new year's quotas.

A few importing countries cried 'foul!' The majority were just impressed with the way Hong Kong ordered things within the rules.

The last month of every quota year was hectic. Because all quota holdings had to be committed for shipment within eleven months, the thirty-day export licence allowing despatch any time during the last month, it was possible for the DC & I to calculate how much quota remained uncommitted. These amounts were offered in bite-size chunks to all-comers on a first-come-first-served basis against production of a firm order. It was a bit of a free-for-all but the result was a virtually 100 percent utilisation of the quota.

Another consequence of the close relationship between the Advisory Boards and the DC&I was the impact it had on the elimination of corruption. Hong Kong's textile trade was worth something in excess of thirty billion dollars by the end of the 1970s, and at least 80 percent of this was covered by restraints of one kind or another. With quotas at a premium, it was clear that whoever was in charge of quota allocation in the DC&I could have devised a private pension scheme that would have seen him or her comfortable for the rest of this life and any to come.

From the start, therefore, the DC&I adopted a policy of total transparency and full disclosure. All Agreements were published in full, all restraint limits were given by category by country, and past performance records were sent to each company so that it could check the department's records against its own and query any discrepancies. Where allocations based on past performance had to be scaled down on a proportionate basis to fit the restraint level, the formula used was published so that a company could check for itself that it had received its correct share. Every company was given the name and telephone number of a departmental officer it could contact with any queries or concerns about the quota controls and allocation systems. The only information that was not published was the size of an individual company's quota holdings as this was considered commercially sensitive.

Furthermore, the TEXTAB, being in the trade and close to the DC&I, was a useful conduit for information both about what was going on in the industry and potential loopholes that might have allowed room for malpractice. In the whole thirty-odd years that the system was running, there was only one case of corruption. An English Assistant Trade Officer was sent down for two years.

These then were the various ways in which Hong Kong attempted to maximise the return on its restricted trade, always with the intention of benefiting the Hong Kong company, often with the consequence of exasperating the importing country.

But then again, they were the ones demanding more and more of the same medicine, and ignoring the fact that it did not work.

Finally, it was in the insistence on export controls that the origins of the paradox of the more the restriction, the greater the prosperity can be found. It was not that Hong Kong's prices were artificially high; rather it was that interference with the market by importing countries created scarcity and a new and higher market price.

One other flexibility provision proved to be of the greatest benefit to Hong Kong's trade and industry. It was beyond the reach of the importing country to influence in any way and was widely used. It was also the most controversial, the most maligned and the most misunderstood.

It deserves a chapter of its own.

Chapter Nine
Quota Transfers

From the very beginning of the restraints on textiles to the United Kingdom, it was possible for companies to transfer quotas. The need for such transfers was obvious to all who wanted to see and inexplicable to those who did not. It was the one aspect of Hong Kong's export control system that came in for the most criticism overseas and locally as well. It was the one area where DC&I faced down its critics and refused to budge.

From 1960 onwards, all quotas were distributed on a fifty/fifty basis between exporters and manufacturers by reference to their past-performance in the trade, which it considered as the most equitable way to reward those who had built up the trade and those who had made the goods for export. From another point of view it could be said that these were the two parties who stood to suffer most from restrictions on their business. Some buyers at the importing end thought they too had contributed to building up the trade. They were politely asked to refer any difficulties they might be having in getting their orders filled to their own government.

An important use for the transfer system was the 'swing transfer'. A company would transfer in a quota from a little-used category and use the amount so transferred as surrender yardage under the swing scheme to increase the amount he could ship in a category with stronger demand.

For an exporter, the possibility of transferring quota was an essential facility. Few, if any, simply exported textiles or garments of one particular type to one particular market. They might well have shipped jackets during the past-performance period but now had orders for socks or underpants. They then faced the choice between either turning away the business or finding the proper quota for the orders they received. Similarly, a manufacturer might have orders for dress-shirts[1] one year and sports shirts the next. Again, the choice was to lose the business or find the appropriate quota. From the point of view of the DC&I, it could have turned a blind eye to what was going on. Any company in Hong Kong could set up as an exporter. Consequently, it would have been impossible to track whether the exporter surrendering the quota was the true exporter or just a cover for someone else with orders but no quota. Such passing off would have been more difficult for a manufacturer to do but not impossible. In any case, the DC&I could see no reason for disallowing transfers of quota and good reasons for acknowledging and recording them. The first was that it provided flexibility in allowing orders and quotas to find each other openly in the marketplace. Secondly, transfers of quota could be on a permanent or a temporary basis, providing an opportunity for newcomers to the trade.

With a permanent transfer, the quota and the conditions attached to its use passed permanently from one company to another. As the network of restrictions widened, manufacturers increasingly set up their own export departments so that they could qualify for a full allocation of the entire quota. Exporters *per se* gradually disappeared from the textiles and garments scene. They were not particularly happy with this but accepted that if a manufacturer made and shipped his own production, this was no more than the application of the fifty/fifty rule. There was nothing to prevent the payment of commissions to any exporter who put business the way of a quota holder. Since the quota transfer was permanent, it was in the interest of the new quota holder and the DC&I to register the fact with the DC&I so that he would qualify for an allocation in subsequent periods.

With a temporary transfer, quota changed hands for the shipment of a single order or for the duration of the quota year as the two parties involved decided. However, the conditions of use remained with the transferor and did not pass to the transferee. This meant two things: if the temporarily transferred quota was not used, the transferor not the transferee was penalised; and if the transferred quota was fully used, the transferor, not the transferee got the rewards in the following quota period.

Critics of the transfer system found this hard to accept. They argued that since the transferee had done the business, the transferee should be rewarded. In logic, this followed from the DC&I's own principle of rewarding past

---

[1]   A term of art. The dress shirt is the normal 'business' shirt of everyday attire, not the fancy one associated with evening dress and dinner jacket.

performance. The DC&I did not accept this argument. It pointed out that, in logic, if the transferee retained the benefit of the quota, it would no longer be a temporary but a permanent transfer. On more practical grounds, the DC&I said that if temporary transfers were not formally recognised they would take place anyway because of the flexibility enjoyed by any entity calling itself an exporter. Furthermore, there seemed no good reason to make illegal or drive underground, a system that obviously bestowed much needed flexibility in a marketplace circumscribed by restraints. And the harsh reality was that if the transferee had orders but no quotas, he had no business. The retention of benefits by the transferor was, moreover, an incentive to ensure that the transferred out quota was in fact used and not wasted.

These answers did not satisfy the critics. They next argued that the temporary transfer system locked quota holders into negotiating positions of great strength with buyers and, in so doing, DC&I was preventing newcomers from entering the business. The DC&I took the view that these were arguments for, not against quota transfers. Given that supply had been limited by the governments of the buyers who wanted to do business with Hong Kong (both because they had no other 'low cost' choice and because Hong Kong made the best), the DC&I saw no reason why Hong Kong companies should not squeeze the highest prices they could get from the buyer. Which is what they did. As to preventing newcomers entering the market, this was clearly not the case: newcomers could enter through permanent or temporary transfers of quota. The real point however was the inequity of taking amounts from established quota holders whose allocations had been based on their efforts to build up the trade, to give to others with no qualification other than their desire to get in on a good thing. It could not be on the grounds that a company had a firm order from an overseas buyer for goods. When this basis had been tested in earlier years as a way to dispose of unused amounts of quota, queues of people, all clutching 'firm' orders, had surrounded Fire Brigade Building three days before the release date in the hope of getting something. Many Hong Kong companies had headed notepaper from their buyers, and wrote their own orders to secure a place in the queue.

In an early attempt to assuage criticism about the exclusion of newcomers, the DC&I made the mistake of believing it could do better than the marketplace in fixing prices. It introduced a High Cost Content Scheme (HCCS) soon after the first voluntary restraint agreement with Lancashire was in place. A portion of the quota was set aside for all-comers who could show that their particular product had the highest Hong Kong cost content. How to make such calculations was well understood in the trade thanks to the operation of the commonwealth preference certification system. The scheme was doomed from the start. No newcomer would open a factory in the hope that it could break into the UK market by virtue of its high prices and the scarce amounts available under the HCCS. In any case, established factories could easily alter their inputs to ensure a high Hong Kong cost content. They did so and cornered the market anyway. So that was abandoned as an idea showing excellent initiative and lousy judgment.

But the most telling point of all surely was why newcomers should want to enter the market at all given it was heavily restricted. It could only be because they saw the business advantages of such participation. But if they were allowed entry in some way, why should others with proven ability to sell in that market, give up some of their quotas, which, because of the conditions of issue they consistently used in full, to someone with no past record and a firm order that any quota holder could have matched at the drop of a hat? (A long question but I hope you get the point.)

The most criticised aspect of all as regards the quota transfer system was that companies made money out of it. As with any situation where a commodity is in demand and it is in short supply, that commodity will change hands at a price. So it was with quotas. What that price was at any one time depended on how strong the demand was for a particular quota. For a slow category this could be very low. There were even reported cases where quota holders paid transferees to take the quota off their hands on a temporary basis when they could not use it themselves. On the other hand, for categories with strong demand, the transfer premium could be very high. There were even cases where the transfer premium was higher than the cost of the product itself. When the DC&I was asked by investigative journalists just how much money was made on a quota transfer, they were often disconcerted by DC&I's answer: 'We have no idea. We have no need to know, so do not ask. And if we did ask no one would tell us. Prices change daily, sometimes hourly, so there never is a firm price. All we want to know is who is transferring what to whom so we can keep track of where quota is and do our utmost to ensure that it is used.' It is true that a number of companies could and did make a living out of trading in quotas rather than products. How many and to what extent it was impossible to say. As previously mentioned, anyone could become an exporter and work the system that way. A manufacturer might also rely on selling rather than making, but with overheads, machinery and workers to pay, it is unlikely that he could do so on a regular basis as a viable alternative to manufacturing itself. There were also a number of brokers in the market who served the useful purpose of bringing orders and quotas together.

Some years into the restraints an effort was made to reduce and regulate the practice of companies doing nothing but selling quotas instead of manufacturing goods themselves. It was a clear sop to public misunderstanding of the benefits of the transfer system and of the ability of the market to find a way round any control. Under the quota trading rules that were introduced, any company that consistently transferred quotas on a temporary basis in three consecutive years to an extent greater than 50 percent of its quota holdings, would forfeit all its quota holdings. In all the time these particular rules were in place, only one company was penalised and had its quotas removed. This company then petitioned the Governor, won its appeal and had its quotas restored. Everybody else could find a way to beat the 'improved' system, if they had to. And good luck to them since they were responding to market needs and overall, Hong Kong was using all its quotas, which was the Hong Kong government's main concern.

Someone suggested that the whole problem could be solved by registering exporters in the same way as manufacturers had to be registered. That could not work. First, manufacturers were registered for a different reason, namely, to qualify for Certificates of Origin for the goods they produced. Secondly, the DC&I, with the help of the Business Registration Office, did a trawl through a sample number of Memorandum and Articles of Association of companies registered in Hong Kong. It found that all of them used a standard format listing hundreds of activities, empowering the company to do virtually anything at all. Inevitably, this included exporting. So, every company in Hong Kong would have to be registered, which would be an impossible task, and it would serve no purpose anyway since registration would make 'quota farming' legal as the company would be operating as an exporter.

Critics of the transfer system (many of them, no doubt, holders of shares on the local stock market) and overseas buyers raged about such practices, and warned that Hong Kong would price itself out of the market. Such claims were, of course, nonsensical. Hong Kong could never price itself out of the market if it wanted the business, which it did, in order to meet the utilisation conditions of quota allocation. It got worse (for the critic) or better still (for the quota holder) because where transfer premiums were high, the holder had the choice either of making the goods himself or of selling the quota. Those that chose to make the goods themselves were then able to increase the price they charged their buyers by an amount equal to the quota premium, that is, the value of the alternative use to which the quota could be put, namely, selling it.

The final clincher, which the critics could never explain away, was that every year, with one notable exception, the overall restraint limit for every country was filled 99.9%. Somebody must have been doing something right.

One final point, as the paradox of restrictions creating wealth became increasingly apparent, the quota system in general and the transfer system in particular made fortunes for a number of people.

Hong Kong's manufacturing costs were low thanks to the wide choice of raw materials and other components that were available arising from Hong Kong's free port status and to the efficiency of its manufacturing operations and import and export logistics. The selling price, on the other hand, was dictated entirely by market forces, and, in particular, DC&I's encouragement to use the quota fully, the strength of demand and the limitation on supply. The margin between cost and selling price, therefore, could be very wide. This inevitably gave rise to claims that the system created a plutocracy and that Labour, as a factor of production, did not share in the benefits conferred by the unique situation in which others had placed Hong Kong.

I am aware this view persists to this day. As one who departed Hong Kong's shores some twenty years ago but remains an irregular visitor, I am hardly in a position to comment. All I can say is that at the time of which I write, things were somewhat different from today. The government had successfully housed hundreds of thousands of homeless people, created an environment where they were at liberty to do as they pleased within the rule of law, where there was no unemployment and pressures on the government to allow in guest workers and where the man on the Kowloon omnibus in 1989 was demonstrably better off than his counterpart of some forty years earlier. If pressed, I would suggest that whatever the situation today, it is no different from the situation that has always applied to Hong Kong as adumbrated in the Prologue — it has to accept and adapt to the circumstances in which it finds itself at any particular time. To go beyond that would be to move outside the range and purpose of this book.

Chapter Ten
Renewing the MFA, Again and Again

The LTA stated categorically that it was 'intended to deal with the special problems of cotton textiles' and was 'not to be considered as lending itself to application in other fields'. President Nixon must have missed that bit because, as this story has revealed, Hong Kong, along with South Korea, Japan and Taiwan were obliged to volunteer comprehensive restraints on exports of man-made fibres and wool, and then, eventually, sign up for the MFA in 1974.

Bill Dorward had represented Hong Kong and I had had to implement the results. The 1974 Agreement had, in many respects, worked well — I have reported how we managed to reach an agreement with the USA in four days. Protectionists in the USA and the European Community thought it had not worked at all. They pressed for another renewal and, in 1977, they were demanding even more restrictions.

Peter Tsao was Hong Kong's Chief Trade Negotiator in 1977 and I was part of the team as the Hong Kong man in Geneva. It was only thanks to Hong Kong that the MFA got renewed at all in that year. The EEC had made it a condition for the renewal of the MFA in 1978 that it wanted, first, 'stabilisation of the rate of penetration of (LDCs'[1]) imports by comparison with 1976 levels' (i.e. no growth); secondly, more favourable treatment for the smaller LDC exporting countries and newcomers to the market, at the expense of the major 'dominant suppliers' (i.e. cut-backs on Hong Kong so the amounts could be given to other LDCs) and thirdly, the EEC wanted all these things signed, sealed and delivered by means of bilateral agreements before the renewed MFA came into

---

[1]   Because frequent references to developing and developed countries can confuse (and cause reader fatigue), hereafter, in this chapter, I use the shorthand 'LDCs' for 'less developed countries' (the original description used for developing countries, but now considered politically incorrect).

force (so either there would be no actual rules to govern the negotiations or, if there were, they would be those of the pre-1978 MFA which they were claiming did not work). For the EEC, the dominant suppliers were Hong Kong, South Korea, Macau, and Taiwan. It is easy to see why. First, Hong Kong: the UK was not going to protest, having already intensified restrictions on its dependent territory for the preceding twenty-three years. Secondly, South Korea: the USA was not going to protest despite its political support for South Korea; its protectionist textile lobbies would never have stood for that, and, if anything, were pushing the US Administration to emulate the EEC. Thirdly, Macau: there were thirteen countries with higher textiles exports to the EEC than this tiny Portuguese enclave on the coast of southern China, but it was close (forty miles) to Hong Kong, and Portugal was seeking to join the Common Market. Finally there was Taiwan: it had no GATT rights, was not a participating country in the MFA; its only political support came from the USA whose political lobbies viewed the place as an even greater threat than South Korea. It was political bullying of the worst kind.

All of the EEC's terms were outrageous but who was willing to take on the EEC? The USA? Not likely; with its own protectionist lobbies clamouring for the same conditions. Other developed countries? Highly unlikely; they claimed to have the same problems and were happy to hang on to the coat-tails of the big boys to solve them. The LDCs? They could protest (and did) but none was in a position to put its industry at risk of reprisals, and, truth to tell, Hong Kong was a bit uppity and a share of its quotas would be very nice, thank you. So, Hong Kong was not only the most vulnerable — with 60 percent of its export earnings at risk — but also friendless, and subject to enormous pressures from all sides to give way to the EEC and save world trade in textiles and clothing. To top it all, the United Kingdom, as an EEC member, was party to these demands. The Governor of Hong Kong rained telegrams on London but the only response was a number of weeping crocodiles while the vultures waited for the kill. Peter Tsao had a very tough time and TEXTAB was extremely nervous about the outcome. Hong Kong held out to the last minute trying to find some compromise. The EEC was forced to back down on some of its demands, but with everything else in place for a renewed MFA, the negotiations reached a stage where the only stumbling block was the EEC's refusal to sign up unless Hong Kong capitulated. In the end, a notorious compromise was reached. In the Protocol of Extension, dated 14 December 1977, some weasel words were inserted to the effect that the 'pressing import problems' of one importing participant were to be resolved bilaterally '... with a view to reaching a mutually acceptable solution ... which does include the possibility of jointly agreed reasonable departures from particular elements (of the MFA) in particular cases'.

In September 1977, I had been recalled to Hong Kong from Geneva to be informed that the DC&I had been converted into a 'super'-department, comprising the three separate Trade, Industry, and Customs and Excise departments. I was now Director of Trade and head of the Trade Department. I was also asked to double up in the role of Chief Trade Negotiator as well. This meant that I was left to deal with the aftermath of the 'reasonable departures' provision. My new department did not cover itself in glory.

I was to find that the EEC's idea of 'reasonable departures' was to cut back Hong Kong's access rights in four categories to below 1976 levels of trade, in one case by 32.3 percent. That category was woven cotton fabrics, the very item with which Hong Kong had 'helped' Lancashire some twenty years previously. The EEC and the USA both cut growth and flexibility provisions. Even Finland got in on the act and reduced the swing margin to 1 percent. The EEC had sought to justify its cut-backs on the quotas of the dominant LDC suppliers, namely Hong Kong, South Korea, Macau and Taiwan, in order to redistribute them to small LDC exporters and newcomers. This, in itself, was a flagrant breach of the MFA since imports from a small LDC exporter or a newcomer could not, by definition, be disruptive. In the event, for knitted sweaters, for example, a major export item for Hong Kong, imports into the EEC from the LDCs minus Hong Kong, South Korea, and Taiwan decreased by nearly 10 percent while imports from developed countries increased by over 2 percent. As regards woven blouses, imports from LDCs into the EEC, minus Hong Kong and the other dominant suppliers, declined by nearly 11 percent while imports from developed countries increased by almost 29 percent.[2] Such cynical disregard of the facts was just one of the many situations Hong Kong had to face with the EEC.

Things were little better with the USA. After several rounds of negotiations between July 1979 and January 1980, Hong Kong gave up carryover and carry forward in ten categories. It also accepted a reduction in the swing margin to 5 percent and a total reduction in access rights of 31 million square yards equivalent. These cuts arose from the requirements of the US Administration Textile

---

[2]   Source: Eurostat.

Program, commonly known as the White Paper, which was a thinly disguised apologia for the USA's 'reasonable departures' from the MFA. More of this infamous document later. Once again, at the end of the day, Hong Kong had been obliged to sign up for some trade rather than none.

Come 1981 and the MFA was up for renewal again. This time, I had to renegotiate the Arrangement *and* implement the results in the certain knowledge that the developed countries' medicine was not curing their supposed ailments despite eight years of treatment, while their only solution was more of the same, but in heavier doses. I have been re-reading the notes that I made at the time of the renewal of the MFA in 1981 and the negotiations with the USA and EEC that followed. I had forgotten how thorough we were. Our approach to any international negotiation, such as the renewal of the MFA, was always the same: first establish the facts; secondly, find out as much as we could about the intentions of the principal players in the game; thirdly, set realistic objectives for Hong Kong in the light of this information, including our final fall-back position; fourthly, determine our strategies and tactics to achieve an outcome as far in front of that fall-back position as possible and, finally, put together the best team we could, in what we used to call the Textile Task Force.

I came across some interesting statistics on the state of global trade in textiles at the time and some comments we made on the ideas the developed countries had for alleviating their difficulties. For the twenty years previous to 1981, exports of textiles and clothing accounted for over 40 percent of the value of Hong Kong's domestic exports. Through the 1970s, their contribution to the net output of manufacturing was in excess of 45 percent. In 1979, the textiles and clothing industries employed about 360,000 people or 42 percent of the industrial work-force. There had been significant diversification within manufacturing industry including within textiles and clothing but it was constrained by such factors as shortage of land, lack of indigenous resources, etc, as has been mentioned earlier. As a consequence, textiles and clothing remained the mainstay of Hong Kong's economy.[3] Textiles and clothing was also one of the most important product groups exported by LDCs as a whole. The UNCTAD's catchily titled '*Review of Recent Trends and Developments in Manufactures and Semi-manufactures: Implications for Developing Countries of Recent Developments in International Trade in Textiles*,[4] from which the follow-

---

[3]   Hong Kong Government Census and Statistics Department.

[4]   TD/B/C 2/204 dd 24 June 1980.

ing facts are drawn, shows, first, over 29 percent of total LDCs' exports were textiles and clothing. Secondly, world trade in textiles and clothing was dominated by developed countries. In 1977, the share held by developed countries was 73.4 percent of the total and the share held by LDCs, 24.4 percent. Between 1970 and 1977, world exports in textiles and clothing increased by over US$33 billion. Developed countries accounted for 68.9 percent, and LDCs for 28.5 percent of that total. The same pattern held true for MFA textile products. In 1977, over 75 percent of MFA products exported to developed countries came from other developed countries, three times as large as that from all LDCs combined. Thirdly, imports of textiles and clothing comprised a small proportion of the total apparent consumption (the amount a country consumes calculated by adding imports to domestic production and taking away exports) of developed country markets for these items. Between 1968 and 1975 (the reference periods jump about a bit because some countries were slow in preparing their statistics or claimed they did not have them — I wonder why?), imports of clothing from LDCs represented less than 7.5 percent of total apparent consumption in the United States, Canada, the European Community and Japan taken together. Finally, while LDCs were significant exporters of textiles and clothing, they were also major importers of raw materials and capital goods used in their production. In 1978, for example, developed countries exported US$1.8 billion of textile fibres, US$1.4 billion of chemical dyes and US$2.1 billion of textile machinery to LDCs. So the negative balance of trade reduces from US$6.3 billion to US$1 billion in favour of the LDCs, not that such a figure has any significance at all in isolation. So, it had to follow that the more restraints there were on LDCs' exports, the less the imports of developed country raw materials essential to their production.

As for Hong Kong, in this flurry of figures, while over 60 percent of the territory's exports of textiles and clothing went to the USA and the EEC throughout the 1970s, showing the importance of those markets for the territory's economy, they represented only 1.5 percent of USA's textile and clothing consumption overall, and no more than 3.5 percent of the EEC market for what it claimed to be its ten most sensitive categories. Put the other way round, someone else supplied 98.5 percent of the USA market and 96.5 percent of the EEC's. That someone was, by far, either their domestic industries who were screaming for protection or other developed countries.

In the run-up to the 1981 renegotiation of the MFA, the developed countries had put forward a host of new demands, and seemed determined to outdo each other in daftness.

The US Administration's White Paper proposed two new measures. The first related to 'surges' — if heavily underutilised quotas in an immediately previous year were added to a current year's quotas, this could cause a surge in imports damaging to domestic industries. The second concerned 'growth of imports' — where there was *no* likelihood of a surge, the growth rates of imports would be evaluated and adjusted annually on the basis of the growth rate of the domestic market. Heads you win, tails I lose.

The EEC was naturally an enthusiastic supporter of both concepts and the fact that they are so at variance with logic and show such lack of understanding of the way business operates did nothing to deter either party from strongly advocating their acceptance. However, when you think about it, if there were to be a surge in demand (the only way that would cause imports to rise), who better placed than domestic industry to satisfy it? Of course, with over 90 percent of the market already, domestic producers might find it difficult to squeeze the extra 10 percent from their own production lines. In which case, they seem to be saying, their fellow countrymen should nobly suffer in order to protect their inefficiency while those able to fill the gap should be penalised for their ability (and having the temerity?) to respond so quickly. To evaluate and adjust imports annually on the basis of the growth rate of the domestic market suffers from the slight disadvantage of not being possible until it is too late to do anything about it. Neither party mentioned the small matter of the rights and obligations enshrined in such things as the GATT and the numerous bilateral agreements each had made under the MFA with their annual restraint limits. Surge and growth adjustment were nothing more than the crudest attempts to assuage the pressures of the powerful in total disregard of the consequences for the powerless, and manifestations of the intellectual dishonesty of those who propounded them. The concept of 'globalisation', was another notion that garnered a lot of developed country support. While global suggests, well, global, the concept seemed to mean a globe consisting only of LDC exporting countries who should be subject to a global total ceiling on their textile exports. What is particularly distasteful about this idea is the assumption that there is something intrinsically threatening about LDCs, and as a consequence, no need to explain why such a ceiling on such a group of countries (and territories) was necessary. The British Textile Confederation, for example, in its paper

'World Trade in Textiles After 1981' (April 1980), thought 'the [global] ceiling must make a generous allowance for access to the EEC market by the poorer countries ...' but the 'advanced [developing] countries must accept reductions in their shares of the ceilings'. This offered the novel prospect for the poorer countries that the more they took advantage of the generous allowance, the more they must accept reductions on their exports. The Congressional Textile Caucus of the US House of Representatives adopted a resolution to the effect that 'within the framework of global analysis, special attention should be devoted to truly developing countries ... Substantial growth potential can and should be allowed for (such) developing countries ... if [emphasis added] the newly industrialised countries are restricted to import growth rates somewhat below the rate of US market growth'. The award of substantial growth potential sounded generous but the resolution did not spell out as to the consequences if the NICs took up the potential. It would appear, however, that if a country used the reward to the extent it qualified as a newly industrialised country, the reward would be a restricted growth rate somewhat below the one that US industry would enjoy. As did the worthy people who made up the caucus, we should ignore the fact that since 'the rate of US Market growth' is infinite and depends entirely on demand, it is not possible to restrict imports to growth rates 'somewhat below' market growth because we do not know what that growth is until it has grown, and once it has grown, it is too late to do anything about it.

The Co-ordination Committee for the Textile Industries in the European Economic Community (COMITEXTIL) stressed the importance of 'globalisation' in its position paper of May 1980. In its view '... in the event of imports [from developed countries] which pose serious problems to the Community textile industry, the EEC should seek the type of action which would lead to a mutually acceptable solution'. Clearly, COMITEXTIL had never heard of the MFA, or, if they had, laboured under the common misconception that it applied only to LDCs. For low-cost suppliers within the MFA, COMITEXTIL said that 'priority must be given to the regulation of imports ... to an even greater extent than in the past. This could be done, for instance, by evaluating their respective levels of development on the basis of criteria adopted in respect of tariff preferences'. They do not say why, and ignore the fact that the question of evaluating 'respective levels of development on the basis of criteria adopted in respect of tariff preferences' had already provoked years of wrangling before this attempt to resuscitate the idea — see Chapter Thirteen. Just to make sure that the LDCs did not take some sneaky advantage, COMITEXTIL proposed that the global ceiling on imports should be revised downwards by an amount equal to the exports to the other nine Member States of Greece, Spain and Portugal who were in the process of joining the EEC. There is no mention of the implication that the accession of three new countries to the Community *ipso facto* justified restrictions into the markets of those countries without the bother of having to establish the presence or threat of market disruption as required by the MFA, a concept almost completely forgotten by this time. COMITEXTIL also advocated reserved sub-ceilings for associate countries of the EEC; for other Mediterranean countries that had not applied for EEC membership [*sic*] and for the ACP states (African, Caribbean, and Pacific). Their combined exports of textiles and clothing were minimal, so reserving a sub-portion of the global ceiling for them effectively reduced access for other suppliers. Another bright idea was to tie growth rates to the estimated growth rate of consumption in importing countries. No one mentioned who would do the estimating (although one could hazard an intelligent guess that it would be the importing country) and what formula would be used, and what would happen if it caused a surge and if it did not, how that would accord with the US Administration's White Paper (see above).

The British Textiles Confederation had an even brighter idea — the recession clause. 'The level of demand in the EEC must be the determining factor in deciding the extent of low-cost suppliers' access to the Community market. It will therefore be necessary to include a growth/recession clause or a similar device to relate the growth of low-cost imports to the state of demand in the Community, with the object of "sharing" growth in demand or recession between the EEC industry and the Community's low-cost suppliers.' The brilliance of such a non-sequitur is rather tarnished by the Confederation's own recognition of 'the difficulty of devising such a formula without inviting the annual renegotiation of the agreements' Which also goes to show that the Confederation did not even recognise the nature of the difficulty, since annual renegotiation of the agreements would do nothing to solve the problem. Presumably, the British Textile Confederation got its daft ideas from its even dafter members because the daftest idea of all was that 'we must also press for the inclusion of a social clause, whereby quota levels can be reviewed if supplying countries fail to observe International Labour Organisation (ILO) rules concerning working conditions and freedom of association'. So, we did our homework on this one. Even ignoring the fact that the idea is completely *ultra vires* the MFA, and without giving a thought to how many countries would support the idea of another country imposing ILO rules and standards on it, we investigated how many ILO conventions some of the major players had ratified. The score-card was USA 7, UK 75, and Spain 104. We concluded that Britain's exports to Spain should be 'reviewed' and the USA's exports to Britain and Spain even more so.[5] Finally, there was the long-standing, widely supported and totally fallacious argument of 'cumulative market disruption'. This was a sub-set of 'globalisation' and a favourite theme of the EEC, which liked to use the analogy of the wine-glass. The EEC argued that its total market for textiles and garments resembled a wine-glass with a finite capacity. Apart from a little surface tension (EEC joke), if the wineglass was over-filled, the wine would spill, and ruin the pristine tablecloth beneath. So it was with textiles. One additional piece in the market beyond full capacity would destroy the EEC's textile industries. Consequently, there had to be restraints on textiles to ensure the glass did not overflow. The fiercest criticism of this theory, of course, came from Hong Kong. Bill Dorward, T. H. 'Brian' Chau and I all had a go at the EEC on this one. My intervention had the additional nuance of coming from three rows back in the EEC's own delegation, the United Kingdom speaking on behalf of Hong Kong.

'I have a number of questions for the leader of my delegation', I began, tongue firmly positioned in cheek. 'First, how was the finite capacity of the European textile market determined, since the ability to foresee demand and the formula used to calculate it would be of considerable interest to many delegations present? Secondly, if the additional imported piece disrupts the market and causes the wine-glass to overflow, how is it that an additional piece produced by a domestic supplier does not? Thirdly, what type of material is used for this wineglass for it has amazing qualities of elasticity? It is clear that the restraints to which my leader has referred apply only to developing countries and not to imports from developed countries. How does the wineglass expand to accommodate imports from developed countries while a single extra piece from a developing country brings disaster?'

And so on.

'My final question is whether the leader of my delegation could inform us if the pristine tablecloth was made in Hong Kong.'

---

5   Much of the foregoing is sourced from a pamphlet 'Myths, Facts, Application' published by The Hong Kong Textile and Clothing Industries' Joint Conference in 1979

The GATT Director General would quickly stifle a grin and intervene to say that these were all questions that needed further detailed examination and invite the distinguished delegate for Hungary to address the meeting next.

It is clear why an essential quality for a really good negotiator is the ability to suspend all belief in common sense and logic, and to replace them with cynical pragmatism and a strong conviction that the world is mad. For a theme that runs throughout these ideas is that 'low-cost' is something to be ashamed of. It is presented as a sure sign of underdevelopment, an over-eagerness to export and a reason to discourage a country from attempting to improve its economy. Following the same logic, the discouragement of improved economies for LDCs was the way to save developed countries from the threat of low-cost supplies. Perish the thought that low cost might have something to do with greater efficiency. I have perhaps over-egged the point but these were all serious propositions put forward to address a problem which twenty-odd years of restrictions had shown no signs of resolving.

Having ridiculed the developed countries' proposals, we were then faced with the more challenging task of taking them seriously and drawing up our objectives, strategies and tactics to deal with them. The upcoming negotiation was considered to be so vital to Hong Kong's interests that these had gone to the Executive Council for its endorsement. The various positions of the developed countries were set before members. The next issue was the position of the LDCs. The feeling was that they were resigned to the idea of another extension of the MFA, and that, as a unit, they represented a substantial force against the developed countries to limit its impact as far as possible. On the other hand, there were many divisions among them and widely disparate objectives and states of development. Hong Kong saw the maintenance of unity among LDCs as of paramount importance, not least, because, having no economic or political influence of its own and unloved by mother, it needed the shield that LDC unity provided when the going got tough. Hong Kong identified an additional seven influences which it had to take into account but which it had no ability to control. These were job displacement in developed countries arising from improved efficiency but claimed by protectionists to be caused by low cost imports; artificially low mmf feedstock prices in the US due to oil-pricing policies causing unfair competition in Europe; mislabelling of products from East Europe entering the EEC because of the West/East Germany dislocation; unrestricted trade among developed countries (mentioned above); false certification of origin; government subsidies and dumping issues and closed markets in most LDC countries, denying access to all on an MFN basis. In the light of these considerations, the Hong Kong assessment was that a renewed MFA was desirable as a safety-valve which would allow the USA and EEC to let off protectionist pressure without resort to mutually antagonistic actions, even though they would be used principally against the LDCs with special attention to the 'dominant suppliers' — Hong Kong, Macau, South Korea and Taiwan. At least the problem would be limited to textiles and garments where Hong Kong remained the dominant supplier.

The factors led to a foregone conclusion: Hong Kong's principal objective (and final fall-back position) was to protect its position, as far as possible, from erosion in its main markets (i.e. the USA and EEC) as a result of policies they might adopt for spurious but politically expedient reasons. This translated into a strategy of securing the renewal of the MFA in its original form minus the 'reasonable departures clause' in the Protocol of Extension of 1977. Finally, as a Trade Department memorandum on the subject concludes: '... the methods to be used to implement the strategy, that is to say, the tactics, will be the responsibility of the negotiators'.

It was against this background that, come June 1981, I was leading the Hong Kong Textile Task Force back to Geneva, and the process of negotiating the future of international trade in textiles and the part the MFA might play in that future, got under way.

The negotiations lasted from June until December 1981. Their outcome hinged yet again on whether Hong Kong and the EEC could find some rapprochement. The final round of talks ran from 14 November to 22 December 1981. On my return to Hong Kong, I had to meet the media and issue a press release. The line I took at the meeting and in the press release went along the following lines. For some five weeks, we had been engaged in intensive negotiations on the future of the MFA, of crucial importance to Hong Kong. Although we had hoped that, as a group, the developing countries could secure some improvements in the MFA along the lines drawn up by the exporting developing countries in their meeting in New Delhi in early November, we had found that as the negotiations progressed we increasingly had to fight a rearguard action to contain the situation and to preserve what few benefits remained in the MFA for developing countries in the face of strong demands from the importing countries. The United States demanded lower growth on suppliers, such as Hong Kong and South Korea, and wanted to reduce the opportunities for swing and to eliminate carryover and carry forward. The EEC's demands had been worse still. The Community insisted on cutting back Hong Kong's and South Korea's quotas in those categories where we were most competitive, on giving lower growth, on eliminating swing, carryover and carry forward and to oblige us to use a given amount of EEC fabrics in our garment exports if we wished to fully utilise our quotas. The Community also wanted an anti-surge mechanism which would prevent full utilisation of quotas where there had been shortfalls in a previous year. After giving these details of the relative positions of the major players, I tried to soften the blow a little.

'In the final result', the press release said, 'inevitably, some concessions had to be made to secure a new MFA. But the concessions which have been made contain safeguards which should offer some protection in bilateral negotiations for the exporting countries'. I then tried to finish on a positive note, 'we have managed to build in two very important concepts — first, that any concessions have to be acceptable to both parties, and, secondly, that the importing country does not have the right to unilateral action in the last resort. These points are particularly important in the application of the anti-surge mechanism and in discussions on the flexibility provisions to be incorporated in bilateral negotiations. On cut-backs on Hong Kong's quotas, we have refused to accept that any unilateral authority be vested in the EEC on this ... and we have, at last, got rid of the well-intentioned but heavily abused so-called "reasonable departures" clause'.

I pointed out that concluding MFA III marked only the beginning and we now had to translate its provisions into the practicalities of new bilateral agreements with our trading partners in the course of the following year. That would be the real test of any success we had achieved in the multinational negotiations.

The press release concluded, 'A final word about developing exporting country co-ordination and co-operation. The doubters who believed that LDC unity was a pipe-dream have been surprised — but not half as surprised as the importing countries who based their strategy on the belief that our unity would fall to pieces at the last moment. The resultant strength that we achieved through remaining united was a significant factor in resisting the more extreme demands of the importing countries and securing a balanced Protocol of Extension to the MFA.'

Behind the brave face of this press release, much blood had been let due to too many close shaves. Essentially, the negotiations hinged on the needs of four main players, the USA, the EEC, Hong Kong and the other LDCs as a group. The USA and the EEC had common goals in some areas but different strategies for achieving them. Hong Kong needed to keep the support of the LDCs while, at the same time, avoiding the application to all LDCs of particularly harsh treatment said to be intended for Hong Kong alone. There were four main issues in contention — firstly, growth and flexibility: where the USA wanted less, and the EEC none at all, while the LDCs wanted more; secondly, under-utilisation of quotas: the anti-surge mechanism mentioned above, where the USA and EEC sought safeguards against sharp rises in imports in previously under-utilised quotas, which the LDCs as a group refused point-blank to entertain; thirdly, cut-backs on dominant suppliers, that is, Hong Kong, Taiwan, South Korea and Macau, where the EEC said it would not sign up for a new MFA unless it had guarantees on this point from Hong Kong, while the USA said that if Hong Kong gave such guarantees, it would require equal treatment and, finally, better treatment for the least developed countries; with which Hong Kong had no problem but the EEC adamantly refused to define. The position of the LDCs was basically to secure the renewal of MFA I.

For much of the negotiation, the USA was happy to let the EEC make the running, and reasonably flexible in terms of how it achieved its goals and on the wording that might be used to secure them. The EEC, however, was insistent to the end that its demands be specifically spelled out in the Protocol of Extension so that there could be no doubt that it legitimised the swingeing demands it was intending to make of Hong Kong. It was here that Hong Kong was initially fighting a lone and losing battle. However, once Hong Kong pointed out that if the renewed MFA prescribed cut-backs while the EEC assured the LDCs it was only intended for Hong Kong and South Korea and Macau, it could and most probably would be used by the EEC against any LDC that looked as though it might be building up some export performance. The LDCs saw the merit in that line and swung behind Hong Kong in support. Hong Kong throughout maintained the position that cut-backs did not constitute a matter for the mul-tilateral forum but for bilateral negotiations. This was the very last point that prevented the finalisation of the renewal of the MFA. Compromises of various kinds had been found on all the others. So, once again, it all boiled down to Hong Kong and the EEC finding a way to deal with each other's concerns. It was by now 20 December 1981 and the negotiations had either to be concluded by 22 December or there would be break-down and uncertainty about the future.

I suggested to John Beck, the deputy leader of the Commission side and a good friend from earlier HK/EEC negotiations, that the only way forward

was to lift the problems from the multilateral scene, where they would continue to meet the solid opposition of the LDCs as a group, and make them
a bilateral issue, where Hong Kong and the EEC might find some mutually
acceptable solution. To this end, I said I was prepared to propose to my government that there be a published exchange of letters in which Hong Kong
would consider helping the EEC with its specific "problems" in bilateral negotiations provided the EEC withdrew its demands from the multilateral forum.
This move served three purposes: first, it would give the EEC what it wanted;
secondly, it would prevent the USA saying 'me too' and thirdly, it would be
acceptable to the LDCs, since it let them off a very big hook. The Hong Kong
government supported this move on my part and when Beck reported back he
was instructed to explore it further. The two of us went to a café in downtown
Geneva and after scribbling over several paper napkins, we drafted two letters
that we would exchange consolidating the deal. There was some more argy-
bargy and redrafting, but eventually, I was able to send the following handwritten fax back to Hong Kong:

'The text [of the draft Protocol of Extension] in my immediately following
telegram was agreed in the Director General's drafting group at 0500 hrs this
morning. It still has to be sold to many others and I will report on this as soon
as possible.'

It was finally agreed by the Textiles Committee on 22 December 1981.

Chapter Eleven
David and the Two Goliaths

With the extension of the MFA for another period with effect from 1 January 1982, it was necessary for David to confront the two Goliaths once more.

The USA and the EEC each had the same goals but not the same approach to achieving them. They each wanted restraints on Hong Kong exports, but their domestic situations, both economically and politically, were very different. I have given some of the trade statistics in the previous chapter. Total textile imports into the USA from all sources (developed and developing) were at extremely low levels. Most of the US domestic market was supplied by US manufacturers who were determined to keep it that way. They had powerful political lobbies. Presidents and congressmen and those with aspirations so to be, took note and made promises. It was virtually impossible for the USA to make a case of 'market disruption' as defined in the MFA. Nor did it have coherent and sufficiently detailed statistical information essential to providing the 'detailed factual statement' of the state of its industry as required by MFA Article 3. All it had was information provided by the lobbies themselves. Much of this was surprisingly detailed; whether it was factual was another question. On the other hand, the USA presented a huge, fully integrated market in which as far as imports of apparel were concerned, Hong Kong was the predominant supplier with its principal competitors also subject to restraint. As the Cotton Advisory Board had indicated many years before, Hong Kong had no commercial interest in winning the battle and losing the war. So there was a basis at least, for mutual back-scratching when the chips were really down. As Bill Dorward used to say, trade negotiations were always doomed to success.

The USA negotiators were nothing but up-front about their concerns. No silly wine-glass theories for them. 'Capitol Hill' and 'This is what the President wants', were the most frequently adduced justifications for any significant departures from the strict interpretation of the rules.

The US team was always accompanied by its industrial advisors and by professionals from the textiles lobbies, but it was sometimes not so easy to understand the organisational system underlying the composition of the official USA team.

The US chief negotiator was always of ambassadorial rank and part of the Special Trade Representative's Office, which, in turn, was part of the White House. (Visitors to my office in the DC&I would look askance and be suitably impressed when my secretary entered to announce with just the right amount of discretion that the White House was on the line.) The ambassador was then accompanied by representatives from the State Department, the Commerce Department and the Labor Department, and, sometimes, the delegation also included the Customs Bureau if statistical or classification questions appeared likely. Often these representatives did not know each other. So, as was customary when new negotiations began, Hong Kong would introduce its team, while the leader of the US team would say 'I'm Mike, Deputy Special Trade Representative of the White House. I don't know any of these other guys, so they had better introduce themselves'.

Hong Kong's house rule was that only the leader spoke in formal negotiating sessions. On the US side, the Ambassador could be in full flow only to be interrupted by one of his team saying, 'Gee Mike, I don't think we can go that far', and proceed to tell Mike (and the Hong Kong side) what he thought the US could or could not do. This was quite disconcerting at first until Hong Kong got used to it and pointedly asked, 'So what is your position on this point?'

The USA was more relaxed about negotiations as a whole. As long as the numbers were correct and the contents legible and in line with what had been agreed, they were happy to initial any scrap of paper, stash the text in a briefcase and move on to the next victim.

The USA always preferred to deal with Hong Kong first. This was a case of testing the water as far as they were concerned. They were reasonably confident that if Hong Kong signed up for something, other developing countries would do the same. They were happy to travel to the countries with whom they were negotiating, and generally, a reasonable bunch of guys. They approached negotiations with a few 'must haves' and some other points on which they could be more flexible. They had an open mind as to how they arrived at a settlement so long as it could be presented as delivering their instructions to their masters and the textiles lobbies. This made for a real negotiation and provided much needed flexibility in producing outcomes acceptable to both sides.

Another feature of Hong Kong/US negotiations was the determination to find a solution, even if it took all night, which it frequently did. On many occasions, talks went on until the early hours, moving from conference room, to restaurant, to hotel room, in order to maintain the momentum and not have to start all over again the following morning. It helped that both sides spoke the same language (more or less).

The biggest fear of the US team always was the reaction within US circles to whatever Hong Kong might agree with the EEC. They never failed to point out when an agreement had been initialled that too many concessions to the EEC could lead to the reopening of the Hong Kong/US package. It always insisted on an 'equity clause' in its agreements with Hong Kong.

Things were very different with the EEC. The EEC never travelled: we had to go to them. They required Hong Kong negotiators to produce formal documentation of powers plenipotentiary, certifying that they were authorised to represent Hong Kong before the talks could begin. Formal sessions were led by a senior European Commission official. Behind him sat representatives of the member states. Only the senior Commission official spoke. His instructions had previously been hammered out in meetings of the member states, with the frequent outcome that the lowest common denominator system applied. The Commission leader could only speak to those issues on which all member states had agreed. Because they represented a compromise of first six, then nine, then twelve member states, it was virtually impossible to negotiate in the generally understood sense. Instead, Hong Kong had to keep saying 'no' until the EEC realised it meant it, whereupon the member states would meet again to agree some minor amendment to the instructions, when the process would begin all over again.

The member states hid behind the protection afforded by not having to say in open forum what their view was on a particular issue. The United Kingdom, in particular, was able to use this whenever it wanted to do something particularly nasty to Hong Kong. (I refer any UK reader who thinks this unfair comment on my part to the role of Peter Rees, the UK Trade Minister, during the 1982 EEC/HK textile negotiation, who consistently held up an EEC consensus on offering Hong Kong better terms in the mistaken belief that if the EEC held out long enough, Hong Kong would cave in.) The irony was that Brussels leaked like a sieve and any country (or territory) worth its salt had its man (or woman) in Brussels keeping track of what was going on inside the Commission and the position of individual member states. If this conjures up pictures of break-ins and clandestine meetings in dark places and drops in trees in one or other of Brussels' bosky boulevards, it was nothing like that at all. The leaks were so bad that all that had gone on the day before was published the following morning in a specialist newspaper dedicated to purveying the news. One of its top reporters, Marian Bywaters, became an effective Principal Trade Officer on the staff of the Hong Kong Government Office in Brussels.

Whenever an agreement was finally reached, the text had to be presented in duplicate and initialled on each page by the leaders of the two sides. The initialled copies would then be exchanged between the two leaders. All Agreements with third-parties had to be ratified by the member states, so at the same time as copies of the initialled Agreement were exchanged, so were letters. The one from the Commission enquired whether Hong Kong 'would be disposed to implement the Agreement forthwith pending ratification by the member states'. The reply from Hong Kong indicated that it would be so disposed. France insisted that everything be interpreted into French, while the interpreters were highly unionised and stopped work at 7 p.m. sharp even with overtime. Any suggestion that a session should continue without interpreters was immediately blocked by the French in furtherance of their crusade to preserve the use of their language and in denial of the fact that most of their diplomats spoke rather better English than their counterparts from the United Kingdom.

In the early days, the EEC had a weight problem in that it measured imports of textiles and garments in kilos and wanted to write its restraints limits using this unit. Hong Kong persuaded the EEC to switch to pieces and equivalent square metres after pointing out that it had failed to find a single consumer who went into a shop and bought a kilo of socks, and just how many lightweight T-shirts Hong Kong might be able to squeeze into a kilo of shirts, especially with vacuum-packing. A much larger problem for the EEC, which we were obliged to share, was the EEC's struggle to meet the requirements of GATT Article XXIV and become a true customs union, with a common commercial policy and the free movement of goods within its borders. Needless to say, a particular target for their concerns was Hong Kong. Each HK/EEC textile agreement had a quota limit at Community level which was then broken down into member state shares using what was known as a burden-sharing formula. While this was totally alien to the concept of a common market, Hong Kong was careful not to grumble too much since it preserved Hong Kong's preeminent position in its most important markets, the United Kingdom, West

Germany and the Benelux countries. (The USA, on the other hand, had just one overall restraint limit for each category.)

As is clear from the previous chapter, Hong Kong came to regard any dealings involving the EEC as a bilateral negotiation even when nominally they met in a multilateral context. This was because the EEC always saw Hong Kong as a special case. Despite the guarantee given to the United Kingdom and Hong Kong, the view of the EEC remained that Hong Kong and two or three other countries did not fit the stereotype of the true developing country. Various names were devised in an attempt to justify differential treatment. Hong Kong, Singapore, Taiwan and South Korea were variously known as the Asian Tigers, the Fab Four (after the Beatles), or the NICs, the Newly Industrialised Countries (past participle, as used by the EEC) or the Newly Industrialising Countries (present participle, as used by everybody else). Such definitions were meaningless beyond the fact that they served to single out the countries involved for discriminatory treatment. What was particularly annoying for the EEC was that some facile justification could be made for discriminatory action against South Korea and Taiwan, who maintained restrictions of their own on imports from developed countries (as South Korea was entitled to do under the GATT). But Hong Kong, and to a lesser extent Singapore, were open markets, and no such justification could be brought forward.

It just so happened that the DC&I system of circulating its top people through the top jobs every couple of years, meant that I was chief negotiator when we met the EEC for the last time under the LTA, for the first time under the MFA (in 1975 — the EEC was not ready in 1974), for the second time in 1978, and for the third time in 1982. Each round of negotiations had its lowlights.

In the LTA negotiation, I found my opposite number was Ben Meynell, the chap who had urged us not to volunteer restraints on mmf and wool textiles when I was working the switchboard in State Department in Washington, in 1968. In 1975, at the conclusion of the negotiations, the two sides had assembled before an imposing array of member state representatives and Commission officials to initial the text. This was a big occasion. Hong Kong had at last agreed. As the Hong Kong team entered the room, Ambassador Tran van Thinh, the leader of the EEC team, took me aside. He said that one member state was still unhappy with the deal that had been struck, and wanted one additional restraint on piece-goods. I was not happy with this last minute change after what had been several rounds of brutal negotiation, and demanded to know which member state was putting nine months of hard work and four years of future restraint at risk. An embarrassed Tran admitted it was the United Kingdom. I refused to proceed with the initialling and called Hong Kong to report. I was instructed to initial. In 1978, after Hong Kong had agreed to accept cut-backs on its quotas for redistribution to other LDCs in order to save the renewal of the MFA, the EEC thought it was on an easy wicket. It had assumed Hong Kong would quickly sign and that would be that. Before the plenary session began, there had been informal talks between Tran van Thinh and me. Tran showed me the size and nature of the cut-backs the EEC wanted. I had been warned that these would be severe. They were totally unacceptable to Hong Kong and way beyond the numbers that had been bandied about in earlier discussions in Geneva.

'We have some room for manoeuvre', said Tran.

'I have not come to Brussels to negotiate how much of what I am fully entitled to, I shall be allowed to keep', I said, 'and I suggest you make this clear to the member states'.

The first formal session began. There was a packed house. All the member states were represented. There must have been sixty people at least across the table facing Hong Kong's customary six. After the usual exchange of courtesies, Ambassador Tran announced that the EEC had agreed its final position for the negotiations. He handed the Hong Kong side a list of categories and the amounts to be cut. It was the same as he had shown me previously. I looked at it.

'I am not sure whether you have reached a final position or not', I said. 'However, I would like to suggest that you change it, because it is totally unacceptable to Hong Kong as it stands. We feel we have been invited to Brussels under some misapprehension. As a consequence, I shall be returning with my delegation to Hong Kong tomorrow, ready to return here for talks when you have something reasonable to say to us. Good afternoon.'

With that, the Hong Kong delegation got up, and walked out and we left the next day for home. Consternation is possibly the least emotive and most polite of the terms used to describe the reactions this walkout caused. The member states had never been treated like this before. Telegrams flew between the FCO and the Governor. Hong Kong stood firm. Either the EEC changed its position and revealed its bottom line from the beginning, or all deals were off. Hong Kong was not prepared to make concessions on other aspects of the Agreement in order to gain acceptance of amounts that the EEC intended to give it anyway.

The Governor personally backed the line the Hong Kong delegation had taken and everyone waited to see who would blink first. TEXTAB was extremely nervous, fearing that twenty years of crafted increments in quota were about to disappear forever. A week later, the Hong Kong delegation was back in Brussels. The EEC had caved in. We were greeted on arrival at our hotel by a new EEC team. Ambassador Tran had stepped aside and put my old friend, John Beck, in charge of the EEC side. He handed over a new list of numbers, and gave full details of the revised negotiating brief he had been handed by the member states. Hong Kong said it was prepared to negotiate on that basis, and, eventually, agreement was reached. But the toughest negotiation of all was that of 1982. This was because I found myself not only negotiating with the EEC in Brussels but with the Financial Secretary in Hong Kong.

The EEC position whilst thoroughly illegal was relatively straight forward. There were four main demands: cut-backs of 12.5 percent in Hong Kong's largest garment categories, the elimination of all flexibility provisions, the non-sensical surge mechanism and the unilateral right to debit Hong Kong's quotas if it discovered Hong Kong circumventing the agreement through re-routing or transhipment. To us, this was bread and butter stuff. We were confident that we could find reasonable solutions to all of them except the first, cut-backs.

Coincidentally, Hong Kong had decided that John Bembridge should be brought into the government as Financial Secretary from the private sector. He had replaced Philip Haddon-Cave, who had been promoted to Chief Secretary. Bembridge may well have been a scion of the local *hongs* and an outstanding public officer in discharging his other government responsibilities, but in terms of his relationship with DC&I, he was a disaster. At our first getting to know you meeting in his office (DC&I senior staff and the Financial Secretary and his staff), he made clear that things were going to be done differently in future. They certainly were. Up to the departure of Haddon-Cave, the DC&I had worked closely with and received total support from the Financial Secretary's Office, not least because Haddon-Cave understood the issues involved and had not only launched the new look DC&I back in the 1960s, but had himself been the Chief Trade Negotiator. It soon became obvious that Bembridge did not know his warp from his weft. The USA had made clear to us that if we gave in to EEC demands for a 12.5 percent cut-back on the restraint levels in our eight largest garment categories to the EEC, it would reopen the HK/USA Agreement that we had recently negotiated with the USA and demand similar cut-backs. The EEC insisted that we must reach agreement with the

Community by 24 September 1982 otherwise it would withdraw from the MFA completely and impose import controls. Bembridge took them at their word. This was serious business with the livelihood of thousands engaged in the textiles trade and industry and billions of dollars of trade at stake.

In DC&I we had prepared our objectives, strategy and tactics as usual and had them endorsed by TEXTAB and blessed by EXCO. Progress in the talks with the EEC was exceedingly slow. Hong Kong refused to make any concessions to the EEC's illegal demands for cut-backs. Word began to reach us in Brussels that the Financial Secretary was 'getting restless at the lack of progress'. Very encouraging when we had been fighting hard in accordance with our approved strategy to block progress towards what would have been a disaster for Hong Kong. When two rounds of talks failed to produce anything of note, the new Financial Secretary (FS) became very unhappy indeed. I received a message that he had telephoned the DC&I to say that two TEXTAB members had been to see him. Their view was that 'the whole of TEXTAB had come to the view that the situation in Europe was so bad that Hong Kong should reach a settlement with the EEC during the next round of negotiations …'. The FS went on that 'if the Board was unanimous in wanting the Government to accept a deal, he could see no reason why Government should not accept it'. Whilst I was ready to accept that Bembridge could see no reason, TEXTAB's purported views came as something of a surprise as only the previous week it had endorsed the line we had been taking with the EEC.

Bembridge's attitude displayed a complete lack of understanding of the complex way in which the EEC worked, how we had to accommodate those workings in the way we advanced our cause, the fact that the TEXTAB always got a little nervous when things looked bad, the importance of keeping the LDCs together so that the EEC was meeting resistance on all fronts to its proposals, not only from Hong Kong, and why I had not called for revised instructions in the light of the impasse that had been reached. The FS's impatience and failure to understand what was involved was putting everything at risk. We agreed to resume talks with the EEC on 15 September 1982 with the EEC constantly reminding us of the dire consequences if agreement was not reached by 24 September. As we prepared for battle, it became clear the FS had not yet got the message. I received the following instruction from the FS: '… whatever the outcome of the next round of negotiation to be held from 15 September 1982, *it must not end on high drama*'. You may wonder, as did I, what this additional instruction actually meant. So, I asked. Fortunately, someone with more sense than I turned my memo round before it reached the FS suggesting that if I remained happy with my original instructions, I just get on with it. I then received another memo informing me that the Acting Governor (Philip Haddon-Cave) had interpreted the reference to 'high drama' to mean that we should not appear to the outside world as an 'apparent leader and provoker of actions and statements which might, at this sensitive time, cause a degree of irritation which could adversely influence wider political issues'. As if we would. (This was a veiled reference to the impending visit of Mrs Thatcher on her way to handbagging China on the future of Hong Kong.)As usual, the whizz-kids in our team found a solution to the cut-back problem. Although complicated in the detail because of burden-sharing and member state break-downs, its essence was simple: while 1980 had been a record year for Hong Kong, the level of exports of garments to the EEC had fallen away sharply in 1981 and in 1982, resulting in, for once, heavily under-utilised quota limits. Thus, any reductions to the quota limits would, in effect, be cutting empty space rather than actual trade; while if we could secure new quota limits at the 1980 levels of trade, we would be better off in trade terms than in 1981 or 1982. Of course, we would be reducing future access rights when trade picked up but that was the future; we needed a solution for the here and now (or there and then). The beauty of this solution was threefold: first, the EEC would have secured its cut-backs; second, we would have preserved our best trade levels ever and, third, we would have a defence against any USA attempt to reopen the HK/USA Agreement by pointing out that our agreement with the EEC locked us into the best annual performance we had ever had with the EEC, and asking if the USA was prepared to offer us the same deal. On top of all that, we had been able to push the EEC from its position on no flexibility so by the time we added in growth, swing, carryover and carry forward, the actual cut-back on the previous quota limits totalled as little as 1 percent.

The complexities were well understood by the DC&I and TEXTAB; they were not so well understood by the member states and certain sectors of the Hong Kong government. It was understandable therefore, that the member states, respectful of Hong Kong's ability to come up with solutions and suspicious that, yet again, we would somehow emerge smelling of roses, would take some pushing towards this solution, and pushing took time. What was completely inexplicable was the reluctance of the Financial Secretary to authorise us to proceed on this basis. The consequence was an increasingly polite but pointed exchange of telegrams between me and the Financial Secretary.

First I was told that I had to reach agreement by 24 September whatever the position reached at that time. This was nonsense because the EEC had asked us to initial a memorandum recording the progress that had been made on other issues by that date, which was a clear indication that the Commission was considering continuing the negotiation if it could. To insist to the EEC that we wanted to surrender instead, there and then, would have made us look ridiculous and undone twenty years of hard fighting to secure and preserve our access rights in the EEC. As we had expected, 24 September 1982 came and passed. The EEC suspended the negotiations as it said it would because we had failed to reach agreement. We said Hong Kong was willing to resume the talks at any time. As we expected, the Commission approached us again, this time for a secret meeting to discuss how we might move forward. This meeting was held in Hong Kong waters on a launch kindly put at our disposal by a TEXTAB member. At these secret talks, we made some considerable but unofficial further progress. The member states, meanwhile, had agreed that negotiations could resume to see how far other countries were ready to cave in. We stuck firmly to our principle — no cut-backs but happy to accept 1980 levels of trade. The UK continued to hold out against more favourable treatment for Hong Kong in the belief that, in the face of threats of import control, we would cave in and accept the EEC's original proposals. When we told the member states that we had a system ready for dealing with import controls, they became quite alarmed, the more so when we declined to tell them what it was. So, the Financial Secretary gave us another deadline of 15 November 1982 to sign up on the best terms we could get at that time. As the EEC was not ready to start talks again until 15 November 1982, I took some petty satisfaction in asking the FS naively whether we might have a further extension. A telegram saying 'yes' through gritted teeth, is best imagined than described.

We knew, from experience, that we had, at last, reached crunch time with the EEC, and that the next two weeks would be crucial to our success or failure. As a first step, we brought the whole TEXTAB with us to Brussels. We knew that we could thereby keep them posted directly of developments as they happened, get instant advice as we needed it and ensure that others did not nobble it if it had remained in Hong Kong. Secondly, we were aware, again, from experience, that the world's eye was on us, and that the world's press, renowned for its incomplete grasp of anything to do with the esoterica of textiles negotiations, would be reporting daily on progress and scaring the pants off people who had a real interest in the outcome. (From this bunch I exclude the Hong

Kong press who had, over the years, acquired a good understanding of what was involved.) So, we began to feed factual progress reports to the press favourable to Hong Kong while the EEC side did exactly the same for its constituents. This was quite beyond the understanding of the FS who instructed that no press release should issue unless it was cleared by him personally. This prompted me to point out in a telegram back to Hong Kong:

- if we gave no information at all, this would give rise to speculation that we were ready to cave in
- the Brussels Office was inundated with press queries from the leading press agencies and again if we did not respond, this could be misconstrued
- our silence would allow the Commission to make the running and present a one-sided picture
- to await clearance from Hong Kong could delay the impact of any story we wished to release
- as the negotiations reached their climax, the use of the media could be an effective tool in our negotiating armoury.

We received a note to say that the FS had been too busy to respond to this telegram but that we should proceed as best we saw fit having regard to the wider implications, etc, etc, etc. Meanwhile, TEXTAB was being kept right up to date with our progress. It was nervous but standing firm. I had to report to the Board and to Hong Kong that as things stood at that moment, we may have to continue the talks into December. TEXTAB was not happy but reconciled to the possibility, and asked whether the Governor could send yet another telegram to London to press for a more reasonable approach by the UK. The Governor had sent a similar telegram the previous week to which Minister Rees had replied saying that he had mentioned Hong Kong's open market as something that should be recognised by the Community, but not mentioning that the UK was maintaining its reservation against any movement on the cutback question. The telegraphed reaction from Hong Kong speaks for itself — 'HE [His Excellency i.e. the Governor] was not (underlined) prepared to send a further signal to the FCO'; 'our time frame does not stretch to December'; we were to sign up 'whatever the situation which will obtain after the November Council [of EEC Ministers] meeting'. The punchline revealed that the one member of the TEXTAB who had not travelled to Brussels 'fully endorsed' the instruction from the FS.

A further 'explanatory' memo followed this telegram. We had to settle on 'the best terms available', accept 'if necessary a cutback as deep as 10%' (it was clear our solution to the cutback question had not been understood in Hong Kong at all, and in any case, the EEC was seeking a 12.5 percent rather than a 10 percent cut-back); there was 'no question of going back to EXCO to change instructions, formulated on the basis of TEXTAB advice, to extend further our so-called self-imposed deadline'. 'There can be no further delays in settling the issue' (indirect praise indeed since it implied that we could hurry-up the EEC decision-making process). 'There is considerable concern and agitation in the trade' said the FS, rather unadvisedly, in my view, with his advisors minus one six thousand miles away, sitting in the room next door to me; 'the outcome must be one where the Hong Kong Delegation comes back, this time with an agreement', [as if we had never done so before]. These messages were received by us just as things were coming to a head. Bill Dorward, Chairman of TEXTAB, had had to leave that morning for a GATT meeting in Geneva that I could not attend, so it was left to me to chair the next meeting of the Board. I read out selected passages from the messages I had received. The minutes of the meeting were carefully edited for archive purposes, but my telegram reporting the reaction of TEXTAB gave a rather fuller and more accurate version.

I first showed members what we would be signing up to if we surrendered, pointing out that the advances on that position we had made with John Beck and his colleagues on the launch in Hong Kong were all unofficial and would have no standing if we capitulated. The discussion thereafter was lively. This was the only time that I ever saw the TEXTAB really angry. 'We are being told to surrender whatever the situation by the deadline, when we made the deadline', said one. 'If EXCO made their advice on the basis of TEXTAB's advice, why can't EXCO change its mind, if we change our advice on which theirs is based?' asked another. 'If this is EXCO's advice, we may as well pack up and go home', said a third. 'We here in Brussels are the representatives of the trade and should have some say in the final instructions', added a fourth. In response to this reaction, I received yet another extension, this time to 30 November 1982. In all between 18 November and 24 November 1982, we received nine messages saying that we had to follow our (rather confused) instructions. We were able finally, to persuade the EEC to accept the 1980 levels of trade as the new restraint levels. My handwritten notes record 'Agreement initialled 0215 hrs on 1 December 1982'. When I woke up next morning and re-examined our agreement, I found that two sleepy negotiators had dated it 31 November. No slight intended to the FS, at least, that was my explanation for the mistake and I have seen no other.

When we reported that agreement had been reached, we received the following telegram from Hong Kong: 'The initialling of the agreement was greeted in the FS Committee with sighs of relief'. Bill Dorward replied: 'The TEXTAB congratulated the delegation on their dedication, skill, and exercise of judgement. I should have thought the Hong Kong reaction might, at least, have been "well done" rather than "sighs of relief"'.

So much for old hands and new brooms.

Chapter Twelve
The Four Faces of Hong Kong

A major issue from the start was how Hong Kong's relationship with the United Kingdom should and could be managed.

Immediately following the Second World War, the United Kingdom was leaning towards socialism, striving to maintain its pre-war standing in world affairs, and slowly abandoning its colonial past. Constitutionally, Hong Kong was a dependent territory for which the United Kingdom had formal international responsibility and a duty of care as regards its well-being. The UK could not in all conscience offload it to an insecure regime in China or set it free as an independent entity. Furthermore, no sooner had Hong Kong begun to recover from Japanese occupation than unrest in China gave rise to a massive influx of people to its already crowded townships, villages and, ultimately, hillsides. Domestic issues and the political pressures in the UK made things even more difficult, especially as Hong Kong's solution to its problems was to trade its way out of trouble, with the UK as its principal market thanks to Commonwealth Preference. So, when problems between Hong Kong and the United Kingdom on trade matters first surfaced, the voluntary industry-to-industry agreement between Hong Kong and Lancashire provided a convenient cover not only because of the complications that could have arisen for world trade if the GATT, then only ten years old, had been used in some way, but mainly because it glossed over the constitutional and political questions that hung unresolved over each. The introduction of the STA and LTA then provided another convenient escape route in terms of bilateral relations between the two: a set of internationally agreed rules offered a framework of sorts which the UK and Hong Kong could use as a pretext for working out mutually acceptable arrangements. The real difficulties arose in respect of Hong Kong's dealings with other countries and in international meetings.

Although Hong Kong had acquired GATT rights and obligations, their exercise by and application to Hong Kong remained legally with the United Kingdom. In international meetings, there was no question that Hong Kong's views should be heard and that this could be done by the UK delegation to the meeting speaking first, on behalf of the United Kingdom, and then, on behalf of Hong Kong. This latter intervention could be done by someone from Hong Kong since there was nothing to prevent different people from the same delegation speaking on different aspects of an issue. Initially, at least, there was little difference between the line taken by the two parties. Even in such a matter as the GSP negotiations, Hong Kong was able to argue that territories such as Hong Kong should be accepted as developing without compromising the UK's position. It was only when a country wanted Hong Kong to restrain exports of textiles and garments that real problems arose. The situation then was that the UK was put in the position of having to defend Hong Kong's position on the one hand while on the other, it had already secured restrictions for itself on Hong Kong. The only solution to maintain the constitutional and the GATT position was to create the fiction that the UK was defending Hong Kong, each case being treated on its merits. To this end, any trade negotiations with Hong Kong were held nominally with the presence of a UK official from the FCO while the actual negotiation would be carried out by Hong Kong officials seeking to get the best deal they could for Hong Kong. The United Kingdom would then formally endorse the outcome. The UK and Hong Kong had each been disadvantaged by the situation's impracticality and the confusion it caused as to who was representing whom. Was this the UK speaking on behalf of Hong Kong, or Hong Kong speaking on behalf of Hong Kong or the UK speaking on behalf of the UK using Hong Kong as a tool? Matters grew even more complicated when the UK joined the European Community and, thereby, acquired a third allegiance — as a member state it had to accept and follow the common commercial policies of the EEC that were being formulated. Furthermore, the EEC convention was that the common market had a common position on whatever was being discussed and that position was presented by the spokesman for the European Commission and individual member states did not speak at all.

The final problem was the question of China. I have no personal knowledge of what, if anything, went on behind the scenes in the sixties and seventies between London and Beijing as regards the position of Hong Kong, but it was made clear to us in DC&I that China abhorred any implication that Hong Kong was independent or anything other than an integral part of China, temporarily in foreign hands and that we should always bear this in mind when speaking both in multilateral and bilateral situations. As to Hong Kong's part in all this, it was happy to muddle along in other areas but as far as trade was concerned, it had to have some measure of international recognition and legitimate standing if it was to survive. The limited goal of the Hong Kong government was therefore to secure some freedom to operate in trade matters in what it saw as the best interests of Hong Kong. At the same time, it wanted to avoid anything that might be construed as a constitutional issue for the United Kingdom or upsetting to China. For completely different reasons, Hong Kong, the United Kingdom and China had a common interest in the territory's survival. It was this, perhaps, that gave impetus to finding a solution acceptable to all. Once again, the dear, old, provisionally accepted, never ratified GATT came to the rescue.

Article XXVI (5)(a) had already conferred GATT rights on Hong Kong by virtue of its being a territory for which the United Kingdom had 'international responsibilities'. Hong Kong's salvation lay further down the page in Article XXVI (5)(c). This states that 'If any of the customs territories [e.g. Hong Kong] in respect of which a contacting party [e.g. the United Kingdom] has accepted this Agreement [i.e. the GATT], possesses or acquires full autonomy in the conduct of its external commercial relations [i.e. has or obtains the right to conduct its own trade affairs] and of the other matters provided for in this Agreement [i.e. as well as the power to do the other things provided for in the GATT], such territory [i.e. Hong Kong] shall, upon sponsorship through a declaration by the responsible contracting party [i.e. the United Kingdom] establishing the above-mentioned fact [i.e. that Hong Kong is a separate customs territory and has full authority to follow the requirements of the GATT and pursue its own trade policies], be deemed to be a contracting party [i.e. a full member of the GATT]'. By now, Hong Kong had achieved *de facto* autonomy in the conduct of its external commercial relations for the simple reason that the mother country could no longer in good conscience advise Hong Kong what to do. The UK had led the queue for restrictions on the territory's trade and the European Community made it difficult for the UK to speak in defence of Hong Kong, especially if this conflicted with EEC policies (which it usually did). Hong Kong was self-evidently a separate customs territory by several thousand miles. All that was needed therefore was a formal declaration by the United Kingdom granting Hong Kong full autonomy in the conduct of its external commercial relations. Such a declaration would mean that Hong Kong would acquire the full rights and obligations of a GATT member ('contracting party') in its own right, and no longer through its dependent territory status. That settled two thirds of the problem.

The question then was whether such an outcome was acceptable to China. Again, I do not know what the formal position of China on this issue was at the time and the extent to which it was consulted. However, China's attitude may be deduced by some *ex post facto* speculation. Firstly, in the Sino-British talks on the future of Hong Kong, it appeared as though the territory would be transmogrified into a Special Administrative Region. Such status would mean that Hong Kong would continue to be a separate (from China) customs territory, the essential first criterion for the application of GATT Article XXVI (5) (c). Secondly, one of first issues to be discussed in the Sino-British talks was Hong Kong's position in the GATT. After I had taken early retirement from the government and was Director General of the Federation of Hong Kong Industries, I was invited by the son of one of the previous members of TEXTAB to dinner to meet what he described only as 'some interesting people'. I was escorted to a private room in a local hotel where I was introduced as 'an expert on the GATT' to some very important people very close to the Chinese Foreign Minister. They questioned me long into the night on the GATT, why it was important for Hong Kong and my views on how Hong Kong and China might become members. I was happy to oblige. The next morning, I was sitting in my office when my secretary came in to tell me that Mr. Smith was outside, had told her he knew me and wanted to see me on a private matter. I had no recollection of a Mr. Smith that I knew or had met recently, but asked her to show him in.

'I hear you had an interesting meeting at the … hotel last night. Would you mind telling me who you met and what you talked about?' asked Mr. Smith. He turned out to be a member of Hong Kong's Special Branch. So, I told him. I have no idea how he knew, and even less whether my talk with the Chinese officials had any bearing on China's decision to agree that Hong Kong's GATT status should be preserved after 1997 with China making the necessary declarations in the GATT. I thought it wiser not to ask. It was also very clear that China was keen to resume its own membership of the GATT. It had a long struggle with its re-entry negotiations: they took nearly twelve years to complete. In 1995, when I was working for the UNDP's Large Enterprise Management Programme in China, I was asked by the Chinese government to organise and present a seminar on the GATT in Shanghai for some of the largest public (B share) companies. So if there was any problem with China that Hong Kong should fight its own corner where trade was concerned after 1997, it certainly did not enter the public domain. But that was for after 1997. Before then, nervousness about Hong Kong being seen as 'independent' persisted on the Hong Kong side. Again, this concerned appearances in international rather than bilateral meetings.

In bilateral MFA negotiations between Hong Kong and another country, it was clear that Hong Kong, as a separate customs territory and as a GATT Contracting Party, was looking after its own best interests under the GATT. The question as to whom Hong Kong 'belonged' was not an issue. In international meetings, however, where many countries met together, it was felt that a distinct Hong Kong presence might upset apple carts and put noses (1.3 billion at the last count) out of joint. An important but nonetheless bizarre solution was found. It was another *tour de force* by the civil servants who specialise (and I suspect delight) in such challenges. It was a system that worked, and, at last, allowed Hong Kong to pursue its own best interests without let or hindrance. It also allowed the United Kingdom to do the same, albeit, this time, behind the excuse that it had no choice but to follow the party line of the European Community.

The solution was to be found in the four different faces that Hong Kong had to assume when it strutted its stuff on the world trade stage, each face depending on the nature of the situation in which it was operating: international meetings, plurilateral groupings, bilateral discussions or Textiles Surveillance Body's gatherings.

The principal multilateral negotiations as far as textiles and garments were concerned were those that resulted in the Arrangement Regarding International Trade in Textiles, the MFA, and its subsequent renewals for further periods. I have already described these in previous chapters. This is not to belittle the efforts that went into the multilateral cotton agreements, the Short-Term Arrangement (STA) and Long-Term Arrangement (LTA), but it was the MFA that was to have the greatest impact for the longest time on international trade in textiles. It was essential that Hong Kong play a full part in such negotiations both because of its predominance in the field of textiles and because of its dependence on them. The Multi-fibre Arrangement had created a Textiles Committee, comprising all the members of the MFA of which there were around one hundred. The Committee would meet from time to time, and when the MFA came up for renewal, the Committee could be in session over a number of weeks. As it was an international meeting and Hong Kong was the world's largest exporter of garments, it faced the usual dilemma of wanting to be heard but not seen. Previously, when Hong Kong attended international meetings, it was embedded in the UK delegation and said its piece in the persona of a UK spokesman. By the time the first meeting under the MFA was held, the United Kingdom had become a fully paid-up member of the EEC, and, therefore had no separate voice at all in the Textiles Committee. Hong Kong, on the other hand, was a full Contracting Party but at pains to ensure that membership signified only an independent voice and not an independent territory. Enter the solution for Hong Kong's views to be heard as the Plenary Session of the Textiles Committee got under way in the William Rappard Building on the outskirts of Geneva.

A hush fell over the delegates of the hundred-odd countries crowded into the conference hall as Arthur Dunkel, the GATT Director General, called for 'the representative of the United Kingdom speaking on behalf of Hong Kong, please', to make his intervention. I took off my ear-phones and switched on my microphone.

'Thank you, Mr. Chairman.'

I began my address to the assembled delegates. Necks were craned to see me. It was not easy, for I was located with my colleagues from Hong Kong, three rows back in the middle of the delegation of the European Community. This historic moment passed unnoticed and unremarked by the world that exists beyond the cabal of insiders who do this trade stuff for a living. Despite its lack of notoriety, it was an historic moment for several reasons. Firstly, the United Kingdom was seemingly speaking from within the European Community delegation when it had been long established that the member states did not speak themselves in international meetings. Secondly, not only was this representative of the United Kingdom making an intervention but speaking on behalf of Hong Kong, which had nothing to do with the European Community at all. Thirdly, the spokesman for Hong Kong was clearly English not Chinese, and what he had to say was highly critical of the European Community position, expounded only minutes previously by the Commission spokesman on behalf of the United Kingdom, among others. The final irony was that for a time, the leader of the European Community delegation was Ambassador Tran van Thinh, a Frenchman of Vietnamese origin, whilst I, of course, am English. Our respective interventions had all the appearance of the 'wrong' man saying the 'wrong' things on behalf of the 'wrong' constituency. In time, when the other

delegates had become accustomed to such a rigmarole, there was much anticipation, much grinning and much satisfaction at the European Community's
seeming penchant for self criticism.

The procedures for multilateral negotiations were well established. There
would be an opening session at which those who wanted to, usually everybody,
set out their wish lists, emphasised the importance of close co-operation (=
'I want you to do it my way') and expressed the hope that the negotiations
would be conducted in a spirit of friendship and flexibility and reach a speedy
and mutually satisfactory conclusion. Some hopes, when one group wanted
restrictions and an even larger group did not. Once all those who wanted to
had spoken at the plenary meeting of the multilateral negotiations, perhaps,
over a couple of days, and initial positions had been expounded (or not — the
EEC usually made its initial statement of its common position late because of
the difficulty in finding one), the Director General would adjourn the meeting
for a few days so that delegations 'could reflect on what had been said' and 'seek
clarification of any points through bilateral talks between the parties'. This was
the code for breaking up into smaller groups and seeing the extent to which
there was a consensus within the group and for meetings with other groups
and the 'big boys' to find out precisely what they had in mind. At the same
time, the DG formed his own very small negotiating groups of key players to
keep track of progress and bang heads together if necessary. The DG's groups
would involve individual discussions with the USA and EEC, with the Nordics
occasionally, with Japan and with a select bunch of developing countries that
always included Hong Kong. The other developing countries usually invited
were India, Pakistan, a representative of the ASEAN, Egypt, Brazil, Mexico and
Colombia. On crucial issues affecting garments, the DG would often speak
with Hong Kong alone. These limited groupings had no official standing and
were personally selected by the DG. They would meet as one group from time
to time. It was in these meetings that the real negotiation and horse-trading
took place, with the outcomes and compromises dressed up for wider consumption in the plenary sessions.

Hong Kong was always the delegation in most demand at these negotiations. The USA and the EEC were anxious to reach an understanding with
Hong Kong first since this would set the bench-mark for the line they took
with other developing countries. The developing countries, for their part, were
always questioning Hong Kong as to what the USA or EEC had said to us in
our meetings, doubtless to see whether some deal had been struck between

them and us that might adversely affect the developing countries. In fact, Hong Kong always reported fully what had happened in its discussions with the USA and EEC as it abhorred secret deals in principle, wanted to maintain an open relationship with the other developing countries and, just possibly, because there was no such thing as a secret in such talks, and Hong Kong would have been found out anyway. These private meetings tended to increase in frequency and toughness as the negotiations continued and the meeting edged closer to an agreement. The final give-and-take was often played out in the last hours of the negotiating period. The Director General had a tendency to time potentially tough negotiations for a couple of weeks before Christmas or '*les vacances*' in the summer, which served to concentrate the mind wonderfully if things were moving too slowly. Plenary sessions of the GATT and the MFA Textiles Committee were conducted in English, French and Spanish with simultaneous three-way translation. Most delegations preferred to speak in English. Some had greater command of the language than others.

When the desirability of mutually acceptable arrangements consonant with the MFA under Article 4 was being discussed, the term 'the consenting adults concept' was used as a convenient shorthand. One developing country representative, best left unidentified, took the floor to announce that his delegation fully supported the concept of 'consenting adultery'. Interventions by this spokesman were always listened to with great anticipation. On one occasion, incensed by the developed countries' dastardly treatment of the developing world, he passionately declared that 'our balls are in their court. Not only that, they have run off with them'! In another intervention he proposed that the developing countries should give the developed countries 'a tit for our tat'. The interventions of Hong Kong's T. H. 'Brian' Chau always drew a full house. The one that prompted the Director General to threaten to call in the Fire Brigade was directed at the EEC, and, of course, made from the third row of the EEC delegation. It began:

'Mr. Chairman,

'Before going any further, I must make it clear that we are now responding to the EEC statement of last Friday. We will save our comments on the EEC's draft protocol for another day, knowing that no thinking person will disagree that the EEC's proposals deserve a second round of condemnation.

'A major problem we have had in dealing with the EEC statement of last Friday is that it is full of comments which are misleading or untrue or illogical or absurd or a combination of all four. To mention all of these in our response and to rebut them one by one would probably require an all-night sitting of the Textiles Committee. To spare members this we will concentrate on the EEC's main proposals. Of course, this does not mean that we agree with those parts of the EEC statement not mentioned here.'

He then went on to demolish the EEC's position point by point.

Plurilateral meetings were so called when a group of countries with similar interests met to see whether a common position could be arrived at on a particular issue. We had first participated in such meetings to discuss the Generalised Scheme of Preferences, but had usually found ourselves in a minority of one as developing countries, in general, saw the GSP as a good thing. Textiles and garments were a different matter altogether and we found considerable support for the principles and strategies that we put forward. The developing countries would meet before the opening multilateral session to draw up a common position. Such meetings were useful if not always particularly friendly. They were useful in that the particular concerns of individual countries were revealed (or barely concealed). The hotheads were given an opportunity to let off steam as were those with little trade and a firm commitment, therefore, to stand on principle. There was always an undercurrent of hostility as between those developing countries who really were in dire straits and those who had made the best they could out of the restraints on trade. And at bottom, they were all competing with each other for a share of developed country largesse. As for Hong Kong, it was envied for its success, doubted because of its relationship with the UK and the fear that developing country 'secrets' would be passed on, and listened to because it seemed always to come out of things best of all. So once again, Hong Kong had to tiptoe through the tulips. Its preference always was to keep its head down and get on with the job of making as much money as possible as quickly as possible with the least possible trouble. Countries such as India and Pakistan (piece-goods, garments), Egypt (cotton) and Brazil (fabrics and apparel) stood as the giants of the developing world with the ability to influence developed countries thanks to the wider socio-politico-economic interests involved. All the developing countries were represented at Ambassadorial level in the GATT. Hong Kong had a tiny office tucked away in a corner of the UK Mission to the GATT and, until granted Article XXVI(5)(c) autonomy, was represented by a Counsellor seconded from the UK government. (It has to be said that these gentlemen served Hong Kong loyally and well but their first allegiance obviously lay elsewhere and their presence prolonged the confusion over who was representing whom.) Later these UK

Counsellors were replaced by Hong Kong government officers. The Counsellor (Hong Kong Affairs) kept a watching brief on what was going on in Geneva. There were similar posts in Washington and Brussels (although this had been a Hong Kong man from the start). There was also a long established Hong Kong Office in London for liaison with the UK government. When a major negotiation was in the offing, however, senior officers of the DC&I would always be present, and in charge. The three Counsellors comprised Hong Kong's total official representation overseas.

It is, perhaps, apposite to mention the role of the Hong Kong Trade Development Council at this stage. The HKTDC had a wide network of offices covering most of the major cities of the world but these were concerned solely with trade development (and, later, industrial investment), but not Hong Kong's formal external commercial relations. It had been agreed early on that the role of the Commerce and Industry Department was to keep open the channels of trade so that the HKTDC could promote two-way trade within them. This division of duties worked very successfully. The HKTDC's annual promotional programme was always discussed with the DC&I so that the proposed promotion of 'sensitive' items in 'sensitive' markets could be avoided.

As mentioned previously, at multilateral trade negotiations, there would always be around one hundred countries represented and one territory, Hong Kong. The participants tended to fall naturally into various camps. The developing countries formed one large bloc that broke down into smaller groupings. One comprised Mexico, Argentina, Brazil and some other Latin American countries. This group also produced the leader of the developing country group as a whole, the effective, erudite and efficient Ambassador Jaramillo from Colombia. Another grouping comprised India, Pakistan, Egypt, South Korea and Hong Kong. The ASEAN countries also had their own group. On the developed country side, there was only one recognisable grouping, the Nordics. The USA and the EEC were too large to be groupies and had disparate approaches to a common desire for restrictions on trade. Canada and Australia pursued independent lines, and Austria and Switzerland floated benignly around seeking restraints strictly within the rules on particular products from particular sources, the particular being Hong Kong. Japan was in the unhappy position of being a developed country but having restraints on its textiles trade and was a remarkable combination of lone wolf and dark horse. Nonetheless, it was sufficiently powerful politically and economically (especially at this time) to be influential and listened to. With such group breakdowns, it is clear that a number of differing points of view had to be aired and ultimately, satisfied, with many of them crucial to Hong Kong's well-being. Because these pre-negotiation meetings were considered very important, the developing countries would often meet as a group sometime beforehand in one or other of the capitals so that a common line could be thrashed out in private before the plenary session. Hong Kong hosted two such meetings.

Whenever these meetings were held in capitals, the host country made every effort to impress and ensure the meetings were successful. Hong Kong was no exception. We would block book a local hotel with the appropriate meeting facilities so everything could be done in one place. We would provide small rooms for 'private' discussions, set aside a day for the Tourist Association to show the delegations something of Hong Kong and ensure there were plenty of 'official' dinners to stretch the meagre allowances that many delegates were limited to by their own governments. Each delegation was met at the airport, provided with 'help-through' facilities with customs and immigration, and taken to the hotel by government car. Those we were particularly keen to 'get on side' were treated almost like heads of state. All that is except one. One lady delegate from overseas had shown herself to be particularly susceptible to Hong Kong's point of view and was well-respected in the developing country camp. The over-enthusiastic Assistant Trade Officer in charge of conference logistics asked the customs officers at the airport to give her 'special treatment.' He was unaware that this was the code for the drug squad to move in and take the target to pieces, including a full body search ....

There was tacit acceptance rather than formal recognition that Hong Kong should lead the group when it came to discussing garments. We were happy to leave things that way. We did not want to upset China (especially as it was moving closer and closer to full acceptance by the rest of the world in such areas as the GATT), and we had no desire to confront the UK directly—its membership of the EEC meant that we were free to criticise it indirectly anyway by referring to Community policies. We could never totally eradicate doubts about how much information we passed to the UK about developing country positions — I repeat, none at all — and we did not want to get on the wrong side of the more powerful developing countries like India and Brazil or the ASEAN countries, who also had aspirations to be leader. To reinforce our commitment to the developing camp, we would, from time to time, pass them copies of the reports we sent back to Hong Kong. As is common in government-speak these were copied to 'London, Brussels, and Washington', that is to say our Hong

Kong Counsellors in these places. We suddenly realised that when developing countries saw this, their worst suspicions would be confirmed. Thereafter, the incumbents of these posts were addressed by name instead of by capital.

Hong Kong adopted yet another posture in bilateral negotiations. It was here that we probably enjoyed the most latitude, because what transpired in these talks was either said for the purpose of getting something on the record and, therefore, consonant with the various niceties that had to be respected, while what was said at the private meetings was very much off the record and rarely found its way into the public domain. The bilateral negotiations between Hong Kong and other countries usually followed from, and were governed by, the provisions of the instruments that had been arrived at in the multilateral forum. Talks with Canada and Australia generally proceeded within the rules until both, for different reasons, went their separate ways, relying on the GATT as the means to deal with their problems. On my first trip to Australia for nego-tiations I failed to obtain an entry visa — I had naturally assumed that nothing but a warm welcome would await this Pom on arrival. I was not allowed to land and the Australian team, therefore, came to the airport and we held the negoti-ations in no-man's-land. Norway, Sweden and Finland proved awkward to deal with and relied heavily on the so-called Nordic Clause of the MFA as the basis for their more unreasonable requests. In comparison with other markets, the Nordic countries offered little room for growth or compromise. Nonetheless, a small sector of the Hong Kong industry catered for the Nordic markets and Hong Kong usually managed to reach acceptable compromises with each of the countries separately, not as group. The most infamous compromise was when Hong Kong, anxious to preserve the concept of positive growth on restrained categories from one year to another, agreed to accept an annual increase of one piece per category for Norway. (The MFA speaks of 7 percent.) The Austrians always behaved like the gentlemen they were in all negotiations, presenting meticulous statistics in support of their requests and accepting they had no case when they did not. Switzerland was almost apologetic. As host nation to many international good causes, it found it slightly distasteful to have to ask for restraints on trade. Hong Kong agreed a one-product restraint for one year, and, thereafter, persuaded the Swiss authorities to rely on the Export Authorisation system. I became good friends with Switzerland's chief trade negotiator who later was appointed Director General of the GATT. His respect for Hong Kong and what it managed to achieve did Hong Kong no harm at all in the international arena. As for the USA and the EEC, they have already been given chapters of their own.

The final persona that Hong Kong had to adopt was as an independent commentator on matters brought before the Textiles Surveillance Body. The TSB was set up by the MFA and charged with overseeing the operation of the MFA, reviewing all bilateral restraints arrangements made under the MFA, and considering any disputes between the participating countries, referring to the GATT's Textiles Committee, if necessary. Supposedly, the members were appointed in their personal capacity and not as representatives of the governments that nominated them. Bill Dorward was Hong Kong's first nominee after I had replaced him as Chief Trade Negotiator, and his contributions during its first two years of operation did much to set the tone, procedures and influence of the TSB. I later succeeded Bill Dorward when Peter Tsao replaced me as Chief Trade Negotiator. The three of us played musical chairs every two years, moving between the posts of Counsellor (Hong Kong Affairs) and TSB nominee; Director of Trade, Head of the Trade Department and Chief Trade Negotiator, and Director of Industry, head of the industry department. This avoided 'staleness' in the same post and kept us up to date with what was going on, home and away. I have described the TSB role as one of commentator. The TSB had no formal powers to change anything or direct anyone to do anything differently. but it had a strong moral influence and the fact that every bilateral restraint agreement had to be scrutinised by the TSB and was open to comment and criticism prevented too many outrageous departures from the MFA rules. The TSB also dealt with any disputes that might arise between two countries over the need for restraint on a particular product.

One such dispute arose between India and the European Community, both renowned for different reasons for standing firm on a firmly held point of view. In this case, India took the line that there was no case for restraint; the EEC took the view that a restraint was necessary because it was common commercial policy. As a neutral, my view was that India was on the side of the angels and the EEC was being particularly awkward. It was a Friday afternoon and the proceedings were dragging on with no signs of a compromise. There was much urging from the TSB members about give-and-take ('We give and they take', muttered the Indian Ambassador) and about how we were all members of the great textile family and the need for reconciliation when friends fell out. One TSB member introduced the metaphor of the marriage and how even newly-weds would sometimes argue between themselves. At which juncture, I raised my flag. (As appointments to the TSB were *ad personam*, there were no sensitivities about the status of Hong Kong.)

'Mr Mills, please', invited the TSB Chairman.

'Mr. Chairman', I said. 'In considering this dispute between India and the EEC, we have heard much this afternoon of marriage, of weddings, of newlyweds, of reconciliation, and of making-up. I am not certain which of the two parties before us is the bride and which the groom. I do, however, have a very clear idea of who is doing what to whom.'

The meeting erupted in laughter. Even Dr. Wurth, the TSB's Swiss chairman who was never knowingly caught showing any emotion other than absolute impartiality, was thought to have twitched slightly. The meeting was adjourned to the following Monday.

Chapter Thirteen
Beyond the World of Textiles

As may be expected with a story that relates to an important but narrow aspect of Hong Kong's development from the 1940s into the 1990s, I have up to now glossed over or ignored much else that was taking place at the same time. This has been for two reasons. First, I wanted to limit myself to incidents and issues of which I had direct experience. Secondly, the development of the emerging paradox and the attention that, of necessity, had to be given to textiles and garments required a focus on specific goals and objectives which, truth to tell, provided an excuse for ignoring some of the other important issues of the time. Nonetheless, some of the problems were of considerable importance and show that shoddy dealings were not limited to textiles and garments.

Take the Generalised Scheme of Preferences — 'and keep it!' as an irate developing country delegate shouted at a United Nations Conference on Trade and Development (UNCTAD). The Generalised Scheme of Preferences, or GSP as it was (and still is) known, had its roots in the desire of the so-called developing countries to improve their economies and the stated willingness of the developed countries to help them.

The whole of Part IV of the GATT, for example, is devoted to assuring that the special needs of developing countries should be taken into account in their efforts to industrialise, and catch up with their developed country counterparts. Article XXXVI opens with a recognition of the need for a rapid and sustained expansion of the export earnings of the less-developed contracting parties (para 2) and the need to ensure they secure a share of the growth in international trade, and increased access to markets under favourable conditions for processed and manufactured products. And so on. Fine words that stirred up a great deal of public apathy amongst the developed countries. In fact, nothing happened, so UNCTAD got in on the act.

The old trade adage about movement being a substitute for action and action a substitute for thought was nowhere better illustrated than in the four laborious years of international and regional meetings that eventually produced the Generalised Scheme of Preferences. It was conceived as a means to encourage trade from developing countries to developed countries through lower import tariffs and similar concessions.

The GSP meetings were attended with considerable enthusiasm by Hong Kong Trade Officers, not so much because we thought that anything would come of them, but because they made a welcome change from textiles and because many of them were held in Bangkok.

The only problem was that the GSP, in its final form, was never generalised but an *ad hoc* series of unilateral arrangements drawn up by individual developed countries; the scheme was in reality a plethora of different schemes depending on the country offering the GSP and the products involved; and the preferences were more selective than preferential in their targeting.

Take the term 'developing country', for example. Logic seems to require that once the most 'developed' country is identified, every other country becomes 'developing' in relation to it. Then again, logic never has played a very significant role in matters of international trade. So an effort was made to establish a cut-off point where the country immediately above the cut was the last of the 'developed' countries and the country immediately below it was the first of the 'developing' countries. Where to pitch the cut-off point then became a matter of fierce debate. All types of 'objective' criteria were considered. One criterion, GDP, resulted in Kuwait being the most developed country in the world. Such an outcome created something of an hauteur in Washington, London and Paris. Suggestions and ideas were bandied about for three years. The fruit of these deliberations came in the fourth year when at a meeting in Geneva, over one hundred countries solemnly ratified their agreement that a developing country was any country that said it was a developing country. This became known as the self-election principle.

Having accepted the principle, the developed countries immediately challenged it once Hong Kong, Singapore and Taiwan elected themselves as developing. Hong Kong was careful to elect itself as a developing territory rather than country, to avoid stepping on sensitive China toes. Once it was known who was 'developing', the developed countries then began to list those products and those territories and countries which, in their view, were already sufficiently 'developed' as not to warrant 'preference'. The powerful textiles and apparel lobbies in the United States ensured that textiles and garments were totally excluded from the GSP of the United States of America. The EEC thought it would show its liberal trading credentials and put one across the USA by including textiles; except that Hong Kong was specifically excluded. France offered full duty-free entry to all developing countries for all the products that those countries did not currently export or manufacture, with a safeguard clause that triggered a serious injury investigation, if they started to do so. Sweden excluded Wellington boots, claiming this was a strategic commodity for them in view of its winter weather. Canada claimed that some handbags were textiles products and were therefore, subject to the LTA/MFA and it would be illogical to include them in its GSP as an item that had the potential to cause 'market disruption'. And so it went on. Hong Kong attended all the UNCTAD meetings but, like Cassandra, its advocacy of free rather than preferential trade and hints that it was all a big fraud went unheeded. In any case, Mr. Heath, the British Prime Minister, was a great supporter of the GSP. Since the Hong Kong delegation could only speak as part of the UK delegation, and was under instruction to get itself recognised as a developing territory, and not to be too unkind, it was widely ignored. Only a few of the smarter countries such as India and Brazil saw the GSP for what it wasn't. When the GSP was finally introduced with the blessing of the GATT, the DC&I duly issued GSP Certificates of Origin to anyone who applied. Few did. In any case, a much more important issue was emerging that seemed to pose a serious threat to Hong Kong.

By the end of the sixties and early seventies, the United Kingdom had, to all intents and purposes, become Hong Kong's domestic market. Thanks to Commonwealth Preference, virtually all Hong Kong's exports were entering the UK duty-free, and business was booming. At this juncture, the UK had a third go at joining the common market. Having been shown the door twice by President de Gaulle, Britain was determined not to be rejected a third time by President Mitterand. Among the issues that had to be resolved between the United Kingdom and the other member states was 'the question of Hong Kong.'

France, as one of the founding members of the EEC, had secured special trading arrangements for her former colonies, especially those in North Africa. It was made clear to the UK that they could not expect to do the same for British colonies, least of all Hong Kong. Prime Minister Heath wanted to join at almost any cost, and membership was clearly in Britain's economic interest. So choosing between Britain's membership and Hong Kong's well-being was a no-brainer. The Six demanded that the UK should withdraw Commonwealth Preference for all its Commonwealth countries and territories, of which Hong Kong was, by now, the only significant user. Britain agreed. In compensation, the EEC recognised Hong Kong's developing territory status, granted it GSP on a number of products that were of no value, continued the exclusion of textiles, while France graciously withdrew two illegal restrictions on imports from Hong Kong, which should have been removed many years before in 1947. And that was the deal that the metropolitan power with international responsibility for its dependent territory did with the common market to settle 'the question of Hong Kong'. There had been considerable concern in the run-up to the abandonment of Commonwealth Preference that Hong Kong industry would be seriously affected. In fact, industry took it in its stride. The restraints on textiles and garments locked in UK buyers who had to assimilate the higher landed costs, and, as usual, pass them on to the UK consumer. Other industries, too, were by now well established and suppliers from other countries had never been entitled to preferential entry anyway, so even with the loss of Commonwealth Preference, Hong Kong was no more expensive than they. Finally, although the UK still represented a significant market for Hong Kong, other markets in Europe and, especially in the USA, had lessened the dependence on the UK for sales. So the sinking of Commonwealth Preference that had primed the pump for Hong Kong's early industrialisation caused hardly a ripple, only to be replaced by another problem that threatened to rock the boat.

The USA requested consultations under Article XXII of the GATT (the consultation Article) to discuss problems the US foot-wear industry was experiencing. This came as something of a surprise to us in DC&I as foot-wear was one of the industries that might have been expected to develop in Hong Kong but hadn't. (Another was cutlery.) We knew that the foot-wear lobby in the United States was influential although not as powerful as those representing the fabrics and apparel producers. We knew also that a number of developing countries had volunteered to limit their exports of foot-wear to the United States. We suspected that the US was attempting another of its comprehensive networks of restraints on exports from developing countries. We agreed to meet in Hong Kong and the USA team duly arrived. We should have guessed something was up, for the US team was accompanied by seven or eight industry advisors who insisted that I, and just me, should meet with them, just them, for a private breakfast the following day in the Hong Kong Hilton. When I turned up, I was subjected to a barrage of complaints about exports of foot-wear from Hong

Kong, told how the foot-wear lobby was going to raise matters with the president himself, and warned that the stark choice facing Hong Kong was either import restrictions or support for the US moves to press for an Arrangement Regarding International Trade in Foot-wear, a sort of the Multi-Foot-wear Arrangement, I suppose. For a moment, I thought they were joking. When I said I was quite sure that Hong Kong would never agree to such a thing they became very aggressive and made all kinds of threats as to what would happen to Hong Kong when they got back to Washington. I was more keen to get back to the relative comfort zone of Fire Brigade Building and find out what the hell was going on to have provoked such an outburst. One of the department's policies, a throwback no doubt to the days of Cowperthwaite, who, I suspect had serious doubts as to whether there should really be a Commerce and Industry Department at all, was that we never knew more than we needed to know about trade and industry — we got involved only when it was really necessary. In anticipation of the arrival of the US team, we had done some preliminary fact-finding. We had about ten companies registered for Certificates of Origin for foot-wear. Our exports of shoes to anywhere were modest, and to the USA almost non-existent. On my return, we called these ten companies together, and asked what was going on.

As we had rightly supposed, there were virtually no exports of shoes to the States. There were however massive re-exports of flip-flops. Then, the true picture began to emerge. A number of Hong Kong exporters were importing the plastic soles and the plastic thongs from South Korea, passing them to out-workers for the simple assembly work and on-shipping them to the USA. There was nothing illegal about this. The processes involved were insufficient to confer Hong Kong origin, DC&I did not care who imported or exported what, except where Hong Kong had some agreement with an importing country, and South Korea was happy to use Hong Kong as a means to avoid the quantitative limits on its exports of flip-flops set out in its voluntary export agreement with the USA. Once we knew the facts, we knew how to solve the problem. The USA wanted us to restrict exports of flip-flops to the USA. We pointed out that this was impossible since we weren't making any. On the other hand, we knew from bitter experience that the USA could only be pushed so far. We explained the virtues of the Hong Kong certification of origin system and offered the following deal: with effect from an agreed date, we would require all flip-flops from Hong Kong to be covered by a Certificate of Origin. A Certificate of Hong Kong Origin would only be issued where the flip-flop was assembled in Hong Kong

<u>and</u> either the sole or the thong had been manufactured in a factory registered with the DC&I. The Government Approved Certification of Origin Suppliers (GACOS) for their part would certify the origin of non-Hong Kong flip-flops (i.e. mostly South Korea). (This is a common chamber of commerce service where the actual origin of the goods is certified, and different from certifying Hong Kong origin.) Provided the US insisted that all imports from Hong Kong of flip-flops should be covered by one type of CO or the other, the problem would be solved. The GACOs were happy with the increased business, the DC&I had only to issue a seemingly innocuous Notice to Exporters announcing the new origin criteria, the USA was able to police its restraint agreement with South Korea more effectively and the shoe lobby never got its MFA. The whole incident escaped the notice of the local and overseas press, and no one ever knew the story behind the great flip-flop crisis of 1978.

We often found it necessary to go beyond our remit of the GATT and MFA to defend the wider policies of the Hong Kong government.

The Nordic countries, for example, never lost an opportunity to point out that SAS did not fly to Hong Kong, and to claim this was due to discriminatory policies on the part of the Hong Kong government. Of course, this was not true: landing rights were under the firm control of the British government in London, and operated for the benefit of British Airways. For many years after my first arrival in Hong Kong, civil servants had to fly British Airways to Europe if their first port of call was London. It was a terrible service before competition from Cathay Pacific and British Caledonian brought improvements. I made a point of ensuring that any official trip to Europe started with a meeting in Copenhagen. This involved flying Thai Airways to Bangkok, then changing to SAS and flying to Copenhagen via Tashkent — a longer but much more pleasant journey.

One of the most frequent distractions was questions about Hong Kong's work-force and factory conditions. It is true that conditions for many workers were poor and in some factories, appalling. This remained a carryover from the early days of industrialisation and the twin problems of people who needed jobs and factories that needed space for manufacturing. I have already mentioned how Governor Black responded in 1958 when the UK government approached Hong Kong on wages and factory conditions. The Hong Kong government did the best it could to address criticisms with appropriate legislation and, more practically, with the flatted factory and massive land reclamations. Nonetheless, Hong Kong was getting close to full employment, which forced up wages and factory standards. A massive programme of resettlement housing was undertaken so that by the 1970s, over a third of Hong Kong's population was housed in accommodation built by the government and financed largely by revenues arising from Hong Kong's economic policies.

Events so far have taken Hong Kong to the late seventies. The preceding years had witnessed a period of much progress and some set-backs.

In overall terms, trade was expanding, quality was improving and levels of employment growing. Considerable diversification took place within the constraints that conditioned what Hong Kong could manufacture, and the territory was beginning to make a name for itself both within the developed world and among developing countries. In developed countries, pressures mounted for action to be taken against 'floods of imports' of 'poor quality products' from 'sweatshops' in South East Asia including Hong Kong, exploiting 'cheap labour', 'dumped' in their market without regard to price in order to secure the business.

These charges are worth examining in the light of the situation on the ground in Hong Kong. As to 'floods of imports', it is true that Hong Kong was expanding and at growth rates that were the envy of many. While most developed countries were happy to measure their growth in half percentage points, Hong Kong's exports were growing at well over 8 percent a year. But the number of markets to which Hong Kong was selling was also growing and exports were not concentrated in a single market. Nonetheless, thanks to Commonwealth Preference, designed by the Brits at a time when British industry was dominant in the world, Hong Kong was certainly taking advantage of the benefits offered by the UK market. It was true too, that the United States attracted vast quantities of Hong Kong goods, but in terms of overall imports into the USA, Hong Kong's share was miniscule. Furthermore, the heavy industries that were complaining about loss of raw material sales in their domestic markets were remarkably silent on the export opportunities offered by Hong Kong that had to import all its machinery and raw materials. The claims regarding poor quality may appear more soundly based, but, again, do not stand up to closer examination. Firstly, many products were of high quality (assuming there is some standard by which 'high' and 'low' can be distinguished). Secondly, and more to the point, why were end-users demanding 'floods of poor quality imports', if they were no good? And if they were no good, why did not domestic producers step in and seize the market? Furthermore, the flatted factory programme was moving apace and all factories built in the newly reclaimed Kwun Tong township had to meet stringent building and health and safety standards. And under pressure from the UK, the conditions of employment were slowly being improved. As to 'cheap labour', while it was true that wages were low in comparison with those in most of the developed countries, there was full employment and the labour force was highly mobile, so wages by definition, reflected market rates due to full employment and a highly mobile labour-force.

Claims of 'dumping' are the last resort of the desperate protectionist. 'Dumping' is covered by GATT Article VI. The essence of dumping is that a product is imported into a country at a price that is lower than the price for the same or similar product prevailing in the market of the exporting country. At the same time, a 'dumped' product has to be causing or threatening 'material injury' to established domestic industry or it 'materially retards the establishment of a domestic industry'. Although the meaning is as obscure as ever, and may or may not be the same as Article XIX's 'serious injury' or the MFA's 'market disruption', the implication of Article VI was that a country was exporting at artificial prices in order to corner the market and eliminate competitors. An interpretative code was eventually needed to explain what it all meant. Anyone who understood the Hong Kong industrial scene would know how ridiculous such a claim was. Firstly, the idea that Hong Kong manufacturers could or would collude to bring prices down was laughable. The competition among them was fierce. No one would voluntarily reduce a price if they could sell their product for a higher one. Secondly, no Hong Kong manufacturer would sell at below cost to make a sale. He would rather go bust. Many did, who could not compete on grounds of efficiency. Thirdly, at this time, it was virtually impossible to find any Hong Kong products on the local market with which to make comparisons. Everything was geared to export where the pickings were richer and the orders regular. The Hong Kong market preferred either 'cheap' imports from the 'sweatshops' of other South East Asian countries, or as prosperity increased, the products of famous international brands. So imported like and similar products generally sold for less in Hong Kong than locally produced ones. Later, in a final desperate throw, protectionists overseas accused Hong Kong manufacturers of 'dumping by proxy'. This meant that overseas suppliers were dumping their raw materials in Hong Kong and Hong Kong manufacturers were then taking advantage of those cheap raw materials for their own products. Even the most protectionist of governments among the importing countries balked at trying to tackle that one.

Hong Kong got little sympathy from its developing country partners. They were growing increasingly frustrated by the tactics of the developed countries to obstruct their exports, and by the failure of their own 'import substitution' policies, which, despite the assembled brains of World Banks, International Monetary Funds and United Nations agencies, did not deliver the results that the theories suggested they should. Hong Kong learned the hard way that businessmen know better than bureaucrats how business works. Other developing countries did not. All they saw was Hong Kong increasing its market share. Yet, it had no protective duties, no 'import substitution' and no five year plans for getting from one highly imaginative development scenario to an even more imaginative one a few years later. At the same time, developing countries were playing into the hands of the developed countries whose markets they were seeking to enter. The developed countries protested that since developing country markets were 'closed' to developed country exports through protective tariffs and import substitution policies, the developing countries could hardly expect reciprocity from the developed world. This was said with a straight face by those who had earlier recognised the need for all sorts of goodies for developing countries in Part IV of the GATT and, later, in the run-up to GSP. Of course, the one territory that really did offer full reciprocity, had no tariffs, no import substitution, and no thought of protecting anybody, namely, Hong Kong, was considered a special case. As has been mentioned, it is difficult to find logic in trade matters.

As Hong Kong made progress so the complaints began to roll in. Many sectors in the importing countries claimed they were affected but, to Hong Kong's benefit, they were not well organised like the textiles lobbies and their ability to win friends and influence people in their own countries was slight. In only one area was Hong Kong particularly vulnerable — textiles and garments. Its garments business, in particular, was booming. It was an industry particularly suited to Hong Kong. It could be carried out in flatted factories, its set-up costs were relatively low, it had a world-wide choice of raw materials that required little shipping space, it was labour intensive and the workforce dedicated and skilful, quality was high, and costs were low. Items could be shipped packed flat or on hangers, and large quantities could be shipped in the new containers that were increasingly being used for sea freight. Importers knew what they wanted for their markets so the Hong Kong manufacturer did not have to worry about design and fashion trends. Everyone was happy, except, of course, garment manufacturers in Hong Kong's export markets and the politicians who were elected by them and their workforces. The result was the LTA then the MFA; the consequence forms a major part of the story that this book tells.

In the early days, the Hong Kong government had stood resolutely by its belief in, and practice of, free trade. Hong Kong should always stand on principle, it decreed, and only make concessions if there was clear evidence that Hong Kong was the specific cause of any problems a country might have and some international obligation required such concessions. In this way, free trade would be preserved, and Hong Kong would earn the respect of the other side, and the grateful thanks of the free trade world. Pressures from London to volunteer restraints, the need for US presidents to get elected or re-elected, the obduracy of France in disregarding its GATT obligations towards Hong Kong, the ridiculous claims of Canada that ladies' handbags represented textile products, Sweden's insistence that Wellington boots comprised an essential strategic commodity and the unequivocal advice of the Cotton Advisory Board that Hong Kong had no interest in winning the battle and losing the war, all served to change the government's somewhat naive initial posture. Instead, Hong Kong took, as its basic position, that it would always scrupulously honour its commitments, however unfair or unjustified they might be. It would then uphold its rights to the extent possible but not be daft about it. Finally, Hong Kong would exploit each restraint on trade to the full within the boundaries imposed by the restraints and the terms attached to them.

Many developed countries had embraced the new MFA as merely the good old days of the LTA and the voluntary agreements dressed up in new clothes. Hong Kong was quick to disabuse them of any such thoughts. It insisted on receiving the detailed factual statement of the reasons for the restraint as required by the MFA, Article 3, and the evidence to support the claimed presence or threat of market disruption as defined in Annex A. Since there never was any such evidence this used to annoy the developed countries enormously, but it provided good fodder for negotiation across the table, and, after all, it was they who had written the rules in the first place.

It was here that the already close working relationship between the Commerce and Industry Department and the textiles and garments industry was finally cemented. The Cotton Advisory Board became the Textiles Advisory Board with the advent of the MFA. The terms of reference were amended by dropping the word 'cotton'. The job of the Board was now 'to advise the Director of Commerce and Industry on all matters affecting the textile industry'. The

TEXTAB became one of, if not the most effective, advisory boards within the government/people consultative system. It met formally every other Thursday afternoon in Fire Brigade Building to consider the latest textile situation and its relevance to and impact on Hong Kong. Where necessary it would advise the Director of Commerce and Industry on how best to deal with it. The advice of the TEXTAB ranged from the establishment of basic principles to explaining intricate details of manufacturing processes in order to make the best of a product restraint, to the implementation and operation of an agreement. The DC&I for its part took the Board completely into its confidence. This worried some other parts of the government, especially where there were sensitivities about, and niceties to be followed regarding, the relationship between Hong Kong and the United Kingdom. The Board and the DC&I stood firm on this point. The TEXTAB said in so many words that if the government wanted its advice, then it had to have all the facts. Successive Directors of Commerce and Industry took the line that if the government wanted to do the best it could for Hong Kong in the long run, it should listen to what the textile industry was saying. By this time the textile industry was by the far the largest in Hong Kong in terms of export earnings and employment. Many subsidiary industries depended on it for their existence. It was very much a case of what was good for textiles was good for Hong Kong. There was only one known breach of this mutual trust in the whole period.

I was in the middle of a particularly tough negotiation with the USA in Washington. The whole of the TEXTAB had accompanied the Hong Kong team. A problem had arisen as a result of a change of fashion. Denim suits comprising jeans and matching jackets were all the rage. In terms of quotas, Hong Kong was very well positioned to supply the pants; its jackets quota on the other hand was relatively small. After consulting the TEXTAB, the Hong Kong negotiating team went into bat with a compromise solution: it would permanently surrender some of its jeans quota for an increased quota in jackets. This compromise had been arrived at within the TEXTAB after some quite heated exchanges among the members as to the wisdom of such a proposal. Many favoured it to take advantage of the massive orders for denim suits that were on offer. Some disagreed. One TEXTAB member in particular thought that in the longer term Hong Kong would lose out permanently once the fashion changed. An uneasy consensus was reached on surrendering some jeans quota. As Hong Kong entered the negotiating room, Ambassador Mike Smith, the chief negotiator of the US side, told me that he would like to speak to me privately. This was a frequent occurrence when a good rapport existed between two antagonists in the negotiating room who were friends outside it.

'Lawrie, I want to tell you that I know what you are going to propose this morning on denim suits, and it won't fly with my industry advisors', said Mike.

'How do you know?' I asked, somewhat surprised. We had only reached a consensus within our side a few hours earlier.

'Your Mr. ... told one of my advisors this morning, who told me. Mr. ... apparently has enough jeans quota and can supply the matching jackets from his factory in the Philippines'.

'OK, Mike', I replied. 'Thanks for the tip off. I guess we'll just have to play games this morning and try to find some other solution later'.

'Sure', said Mike.

I was furious at this breach of confidence, and on my return to Hong Kong marched into the office of David Jordan, by now Director of Commerce and Industry.

'Either you get rid of Mr. ... or find another chief negotiator', I fumed. 'We cannot go into a negotiation with people we cannot trust'.

David made some soothing noises and said he would speak to the Governor about it. A few days later, he called me into his office.

'OK', said David. 'You've got your wish. Mr. ... is off the TEXTAB. The Governor has promoted him to the Legislative Council'.

In the event Mr. ... was right — fashion changed and demand for Hong Kong jeans grew stronger still.

As to DC&I's relationship with the principal players in commerce and industry, it is important to view the situation as it really was between the 1950s and the 1980s rather than through the refractive lens of hindsight. The trade and industry issues that confronted Hong Kong in the 1950s were often new and unexpected. Many were understandable only to those directly affected by them, that is to say, traders and manufacturers, yet they needed some degree of government involvement to deal with them. It was only natural that those affected should look to the government for assistance and the government to those affected for an understanding of the nature of the problem and for inputs as to the best way to deal with it. In this way a relationship built up between the two parties. These relationships were cemented in a number of advisory boards, whose membership comprised the Director of Commerce and Industry and as many from trade and industry and commerce as were necessary to bring a range and depth of experience to the resolution of issues that arose. The most influential of these advisory boards were the Trade and Industry Advisory Board, which dealt with general matters, and the Textiles Advisory Board, which gave invaluable advice in the defence of Hong Kong's market access rights and on the means of implementing the outcomes when restrictions on them had to be accepted. As a consequence, a system emerged whereby in entering a negotiation, the DC&I was armed with a detailed knowledge of the practical issues at stake which guided their tactics, while at the same time, the department brought the experience of efficient government management and operations to bear in devising implementation and control systems designed to exploit to the full the opportunities that a restraint on trade might offer while minimising its adverse effects.

A spin-off from these relationships was the mutual trust that developed on both sides and the impact that this had on combating, and indeed, eliminating corruption. The private sector had its ear to the ground, and being both highly competitive, one with another, but also desirous of maximising opportunity, any hint that someone either in the private sector or the DC&I was acting outside the law, was immediately brought to the department's attention (and dealt with equal despatch).

Another charge levelled against the DC&I was that it was the same old faces who constituted the membership of the Boards and that when someone did eventually retire he was replaced by his son or someone else closely related. There was some truth in the claim but none in the implication that this was in some way reprehensible or based on sinister motive. Very careful thought was given to Board membership by the government as a whole not just by the department. The criteria for selection was that the chosen person should be representative of some discrete section of the department's several constituencies — a Shanghainese spinner, a Cantonese made-ups manufacturer, a jeans manufacturer for the USA, a knitter for the Nordic countries, a European exporter, and so on. Furthermore, the person should be of some standing in the constituency which he represented, and preferably a senior office-bearer in a relevant trade or industrial association related to his sector of activity. He needed to have a detailed knowledge of the trade and of the systems under which it operated. Finally, the person had to be prepared to attend meetings regularly and travel overseas in support of DC&I negotiating teams involving absence from his own company often for weeks at a time. And a he could just as easily be a she. Dame Lydia Dunn went from exporters' representative on TEXTAB to the House of Lords, for example. The proposition that an individual somehow profited from service on the Board to the disadvantage of his peers was a calumny. One of the basic policies of the DC&I was transparency in what it was doing. Not only did this discourage corruption but it ensured that everybody knew what was going on and had equal chance to make of it what they would. As one who worked very closely with the advisory boards over several years, I always welcomed the advice we got from them and cannot remember a single instance when its advice was disregarded or deliberately countermanded. If there were differences they were on issues such as diversification which I have already mentioned, or timing: there was sometimes a willingness on the part of the Board to capitulate too early before the last drop had been squeezed from the other side. The only time that I ever saw the TEXTAB really angry was when John Bembridge began to interfere in the Hong Kong/EEC negotiations, described in an earlier chapter.

There was one inviolable rule — the Board would advise on what it wanted but the Chief Trade Negotiator, as the man on the spot, alone would decide how best to achieve it. The Board members were never present during the negotiations themselves. Instead, the Hong Kong team would make a full report at the end of the day and get feedback and advice for the following one. This had been a tradition since I joined the department and one that many other countries wish they had. They often had to take their advisors into the negotiating room with them. The consequence was that the leader of the other side was posturing for his own people as much as he was negotiating with those across the table and we often had to carry on the real exchanges in the hotel room later.

The close relationships between DC&I and its constituents contributed significantly to Hong Kong's success. That success meant more orders, more work and more jobs. There was full employment, and workers were in a strong position to negotiate better terms and conditions of work for themselves. This was far more effective than enforced conditions through legislation.

Hong Kong was a favourite destination for Members of Parliament 'to see for themselves' (at someone else's expense) 'what things were really like in the Colony'. As a consequence when the personage was of sufficient importance, said personage was invited to dine at Government House. And when that personage was remotely connected with trade or industry, someone from the DC&I, usually me, together with a gaggle of local businessmen was summoned to an indifferent meal and watery drinks by the Governor, Sir Murray MacLehose, who, according to the embossed card that would be delivered to my office at very short notice, had great pleasure in inviting me and them. Few

MPs were as important as they thought they were. Rarely did Hong Kong's hospitality give rise to decreased hostility in international trade meetings or, more practically, any increased quotas. I would duly arrive on time, engage the lady guests in polite conversation and discretely help the ADCs guide those among the invitees who did not know that the ladies retired first after dinner or the direction in which to pass the port. My particular task was to ensure that the stalls either side of the Governor were kept free when, in their turn, the gentlemen retired before rejoining the ladies. There was a natural curiosity to see whether the top man in the Colony measured up in all respects.[1]

One of the most impressive guests to dine at Government House was the Prime Minister of Belgium, Leo Tindemans. For some reason, he and I had established a rapport at the beginning of the evening that continued on through to the end of the party. We talked mostly of trade. I mentioned that I would be in Brussels in two month's time for negotiations with the EEC.

'You have my sympathy', said the Prime Minister. 'You must look me up, when you come.'

After the Prime Minister had left, the Governor said he thought he was just being polite. I had other ideas. Any potential friend within the EEC was better than none. I wrote to tell the Prime Minister of my imminent arrival and heard nothing more. After a week in which the negotiations failed to make any progress, a gilt-bordered, engraved card arrived at the Hong Kong delegation's hotel inviting me to lunch at the Prime Minister's residence in two days' time. On the due date, I paused dramatically in the middle of the negotiations to ask for a recess as I was having lunch with the Prime Minister. Outside, a uniformed chauffeur and a large black Mercedes awaited me. With suitable throaty roar, two police outriders on BMW motorcycles drew alongside, and the convoy set off through the bosky boulevards of Brussels. When I arrived at the residence, an extremely apologetic Private Secretary had to inform me with regret that the Prime Minister had been delayed in Parliament but would join me as soon as he could.

'Please tell the Prime Minister that I think he has his priorities right', I said. This remark was obviously passed on for we had a very jocular and enjoyable lunch when the Prime Minister eventually turned up.

---

[1]   My book editor asked me if this reflected the truth and how I did it. I have given an accurate account but since my methods might fall under the purview of the Official Secrets Act, I regret it must, like the Governor, remain discreetly concealed.

Another entertaining guest at Government House was Lord George-Brown, formerly Britain's Foreign Secretary, and renowned for his passion for socialism and alcohol. At the Governor's request, I accompanied him on a visit to the factory of one of Hong Kong's leading garment manufacturers. It got off to a seemingly inauspicious start. Lord George-Brown sat in the back of the Government House car with his Private Secretary, and I sat in the front with the chauffeur.

'Tell me about Hong Kong industry and your textile problems, Mr Mills', said Lord George-Brown. I went on at some length about current issues and potential solutions. Lord George-Brown was clearly paying rapt attention for there were no questions. When I had finished, I turned round to find Lord George-Brown slumped in the back seat, eyes firmly shut and breathing deeply. The Private Secretary put a warning finger to his lips as a faint smile played round his mouth. As the limousine approached the factory gate, Lord George-Brown suddenly sat up straight, thanked me for a very clear exposition of the situation, then went on to challenge a number of the points I had made. The Private Secretary later confided that this was the good Lord's favourite party trick. There were yet other surprises before the afternoon was out. As he toured the factory, Lord George-Brown, a consummate politician, ignored all the pretty girls who had been brought in to work the sewing-machines, and made a point of having his photo taken with the grannies at the back who were picking and sweeping up. At the end of the tour, Lord George-Brown was invited into the manufacturer's sumptuous office. There, lined up on a table was a bottle of virtually every alcoholic tipple known to man.

'May I get you a drink, my Lord?' asked the manufacturer.

'I could murder a ginger beer', said Lord George-Brown. 'I'm afraid I don't touch alcohol. Haven't done so for years.'

A somewhat disconcerted Hong Kong manufacturer had never heard of ginger beer.

Then there was the memorable visit of a senior member of the Labour Party and Minister of State for Industry at the time. It coincided with a particularly difficult negotiation that Hong Kong was having, involving the country supposedly responsible for its well-being. The Minister began to lecture his hosts on the iniquities of those Hong Kong bosses who sacked their workers at the drop of a hat and kept wages artificially low. He was politely allowed to finish. Then, Governor MacLehose let loose a restless bunch of local businessmen on him. A prominent Shanghainese industrialist enquired how, in that case, the

Minister accounted for full employment in Hong Kong. 'Some people in the UK have no idea about working conditions in Hong Kong, except the nonsense published in the media', added another, along with the proposal that the Minister should sack his advisors instead. Another took this up and said the reality was that the workers sacked the boss in Hong Kong, not the other way round. The Minister, somewhat puzzled, and certainly unwisely, rose to the bait and asked how that could possibly be. Several were happy to tell him.

'Unlike in some countries', one said pointedly, 'our workforce is flexible and highly mobile and our factories are high-rise. As soon as word gets round that the factory upstairs is paying a few cents more per hour, the worker is on the next lift going up, and in a new job in a flash.'

'Our workers are more interested in working for their money rather than withdrawing their labour to get it', said another.

'No Hong Kong worker pays tax. The threshold is way above their income level.' And so on.

A rather less successful point was made by another local manufacturer, who demanded to know how many public holidays the British worker had every year.

'About ten', said the Minister.

'Exactly', said the Hong Kong man. 'You see. In Hong Kong they have fifty-two. Every Sunday is off.'

The Minister suddenly remembered that he had an early start the following day and the Governor intervened to spare him.

Chapter Fourteen
The Tussle with TOGA

I joined the government on 16 October 1958 as an Executive Officer, Class II and became an Assistant Trade Officer on 14 March 1960. As much as I enjoyed the work in the DC&I, my prime motive for changing grades at the time was financial — the starting salary for my new grade was equivalent to that of an Executive Officer, Class I, a rank I could never have hoped to have reached within eighteen months of joining the government.

As I got deeper into my work, I became aware of the divergent views that existed within the department as to how it should be organised and whether it should be run by 'specialists' or 'generalists'. There was a time, certainly up to 1939, when trade matters were the purview of a Superintendent of Imports and Exports, whose role was largely concerned with the statistical recording of the movement of goods into and from Hong Kong, of which a significant component was opium. By the 1950s however, the Superintendent had transmogrified into the Commerce and Industry Department, which was charged with handling the increasing but reluctant involvement of government in matters connected with the Colony's trade and industry. The department was largely staffed by Administrative Officers (AOs), Executive Officers (EOs) and Clerical Officers (COs), but the nature of the task and the growing work-load led to the establishment of the Trade Officer Grade in 1954. Officers were appointed at three levels of responsibility: Assistant Trade Officer (ATO), Trade Officer (TO) and Senior Trade Officer (STO). The top of the STO's salary stopped where the starting salary for a Senior Administrative Officer began. Beyond that, all posts 'belonged' to the Administrative Officer Grade, including the assistant, deputy and director posts. The Director earned nearly five thousand dollars a month.

When I joined the department in 1959, there were about ten 'specialist' Trade Officers. The entire directorate consisted of 'generalist' Administrative

Officers, and there were several 'generalist' Executive Officers, of which I was one. The rest consisted of Clerical Officers at various levels of responsibility.

With the appointment of Trade Officers, the issue then was which jobs they should do at what level. There is no widely recognised 'speciality' for Trade Officers as there is, say, for lawyers or engineers. The 1959 advertisement for ATOs required candidates to have a university degree, preferably in economics or commerce, plus 'useful experience' in a commercial firm or government department; or a recognised qualification in accountancy plus 'some years auditing experience in a position of trust'; or associate membership of the Chartered Institute of Secretaries with 'appropriate experience'; or a sound general education with 'some experience' of advertising, journalism or general publicity work or a sound general education with 'useful experience' in a trading firm or in a government department, if possible, accompanied by knowledge of law as it affects trade and commerce. In other words, you should hold a relevant degree but it did not matter if you did not, provided you possessed a sound general education and some experience. The advertisement also said that there were 'prospects of eventual [*sic*] promotion to Trade Officer, Senior Trade Officer and to higher administrative posts for outstanding officers'. The whole package suggests that even the government itself was not quite sure what it was looking for. The one advantage that was clear from having a grade married to a single department was that of continuity. As the variety and scope of the department's work was increasing but entirely dependent upon forces beyond its control, acquiring needed skills was very much a case of learning on the job, and keeping and developing them to good effect as the department developed. This ran counter to government policy for 'generalists' at that time as an officer would be posted from department to department or to the Secretariat approximately every two years. Thus, the knowledge an AO acquired about trade fairs or quotas or industrial investment might or might not be useful in that officer's new department, but it would result in a permanent loss to DC&I. Government policy also was not to get involved in matters of trade and industry unless it really had no choice. Thus, much of the work was considered to be connected with 'controls': the collection of excise duties, the issue of Certificates of Origin and ensuring there was at least three months supply of rice, firewood, coal and corned beef in the Colony in case of natural disaster or national emergency. The more militant among the Trade Officers felt that even Administrative Officers could handle that. Terence Sorby, the

Director of Commerce and Industry, wrote a learned treatise on maintaining rice stocks in Hong Kong, which failed to capture the public's imagination.

All this changed when Philip Haddon-Cave, then a relatively new AO on transfer from East Africa and the Seychelles, was posted to DC&I. He shook up his colleagues in the directorate and the Trade Officer Grade. 'Controls' became a dirty word and we all moved into 'trade facilitation' or 'trade promotion' (not export promotion — 'as a free port, Hong Kong is interested in imports as much as exports'). He created two new divisions called Commercial Relations, and divided their responsibilities between 'Europe' and the 'Rest of the World', respectively. These were pro-active divisions, something previously unheard of. They actually went looking for trouble so that Hong Kong would be prepared when other countries began to take notice of Hong Kong's success and take steps to deal with it. All specialist jobs, as he defined them, were to be done by Trade Officers, while each division would be headed by an Administrative Officer Assistant Director, whose role was one of supervision rather than specialist involvement. This, in his view, should be the future of DC&I, which he described as 'administrativisation'. Haddon-Cave later applied the same concept to most government departments with their directorates filled with Administrative Officers while professionals would carry out the day-to-day work. This operational strategy was said to be justified on the grounds that 'policy' formulation for departments was the task of the government secretariat while implementation of policy was the work of the professionals.

These moves were broadly welcomed by the Trade Officer Grade which was getting increasingly frustrated by the lack of leadership from the top. The only man who seemed remotely interested in the department at directorate level was Ronnie Holmes, who as Director of Commerce and Industry, had to sign himself always as Acting Director of Commerce and Industry because, through some quirk in the system, the top job had never been converted to an AO post at some forgotten moment in the past. Two trade officers, who were later to make names for themselves, shared different views on Haddon-Cave's move. Bill Dorward broadly supported it; Jimmy McGregor bitterly opposed it, seeing it as a means by which the Trade Officers' 'prospects of eventual promotion to … higher administrative posts for outstanding officers' promised in the ATO advertisement, would effectively be blocked. I rather favoured the idea at first but was to learn the hard way that there was more than a little substance to Jimmy McGregor's fears, and Bill Dorward was to find that his warm support did nothing to advance his career in later years.

But in the early days things were looking good for the Trade Officers. An independent Salaries Commission had designated the whole grade as 'professional' even though the Commission had created another group in which it placed 'assistant' professionals. However, the Commission failed to extend the TOs' salary scale into what we knew as Segment D, where the Senior Administrative Officer belonged. Thus while the confusion between Executive Officer and Trade Officer was removed by the designation of the Trade Officer as 'professional', the gap between the top of the STO pay scale and the directorate level remained. The acceptance of these rearrangements by the government was matched only by the determination of some within it to break them up, notably AOs in the DC&I (out of self-preservation), the Financial Secretary, John Cowperthwaite, (who still felt that the DC&I was something of an anomaly) and the Establishment Branch (packed with AOs and EOs, each for different reasons opposed to the growing influence of the Trade Officer). As a consequence, the Trade Officers decided in 1968 they should form a trade union to promote and protect their interests. Thus, the Trade Officer Grade Association or TOGA, for short, came into being with 100 percent membership. Government, following its own labour policies, had no choice but to recognise it. I was elected its first chairman. We drew up our mission statement, set out our objectives and were generally very pleased with ourselves. We even had a tie produced for us in a local factory: it was olive green with the device, embroidered in gold, of a Roman-looking senator, wearing the toga. At least, that was what we thought until an erudite Administrative Officer, Mr. K. M. A. Barnett, rather spoiled things by pointing out that our senator was wearing a tunic not a toga, as anyone with a classical education would have known.

Meanwhile, the DC&I's work-load became heavier and its complexity such that it was impossible for an incoming directorate officer to understand what was going on without heavy reliance on the Trade Officers with several years of experience behind them. It was this complexity that broke the directorate's defensive wall. First, Jimmy McGregor, then, Bill Dorward jumped the Segment D gap to become Assistant Director, after spells as 'acting' Assistant Director. By this time, I was next in line. It was my misfortune that Terence Sorby, the then Director, did not share my assessment of my readiness for greatness. Then, by an accident of timing, Sir John Cowperthwaite went on leave as did Terence Sorby. Acting in their place was Philip Haddon-Cave as Financial Secretary and David Jordan as Director of Commerce and Industry. Both had an understanding of, and were sympathetically disposed towards the work of the Trade

Officers. TOGA struck and formally requested that the Trade Officer scale be extended to embrace Segment D, on two grounds. The first, that it was illogical and not in the best interests of good government that a Senior AO could enter the departmental hierarchy with absolutely no knowledge of the issues for which he would be responsible and, yet, be senior to an STO with many years experience behind him. The second was that two Senior Trade Officers had already entered the directorate level, jumping the whole of Segment D, showing either that the government recognised that Segment D was irrelevant in so far as the Trade Officer was concerned, or that the government was wilfully denying itself the five extra years experience (the length of the Segment D scale) that a Trade Officer would bring to the post of Assistant Director on promotion.

The TOGA request was forwarded under cover of a submission prepared by the then Deputy Director, Peter E. I. Lee, an AO also very supportive of the Trade Officer Grade. It was strongly recommended in typically robust fashion by David Jordan in his role as Acting Director. The Establishment Branch was not happy with this proposal at all but positioned as it was between a recommendation from the Head of Department and a Financial Secretary who had long range plans of his own, it accepted it on three conditions: firstly, that the ATO should be downgraded to assistant professional, secondly, that the TO scale should run from the beginning of the old ATO scale up to the beginning of Segment D, thirdly, the post of Senior Trade Office should disappear, and, finally, a new post of Principal Trade Officer should be introduced. Anyone at the top of the STO scale (i.e. me) would have to 'earn' promotion to PTO. I thought the downgrading of the ATO should be resisted but TOGA voted to accept the deal so we did. I was therefore the only Trade Officer ever who had to earn promotion from ATO to TO to STO to PTO. I eventually became a PTO in August 1969. Meanwhile, Sir John and Sorby returned from leave to find themselves presented with a *fait accompli*. What their thoughts on the matter were I do not know, because Cowperthwaite was not the sort of chap one had a chat with and Sorby moved to the Hong Kong Trade Development Council, replacing Jack Cater, who became Director of Commerce and Industry. 'Our gain is our loss', as an HKTDC officer put it. Just to complete the picture the government promoted me to Assistant Director in 1971. Each step had to be fought on establishment grounds in total disregard of the job that was being done or the standards achieved. They never promoted me to Deputy Director. Instead, I had to act in the job for three and a half years from 1974 until 1977 when, without explanation, I was promoted directly to Head of Department from Assistant Director. So, there was perhaps a little edge to my opposition to Philip Haddon-Cave's plans to administrativise the DC&I. In fact, the battle lasted some twenty years.

Looking back with the benefit of nearly thirty years hindsight, a number of interesting points emerge. The Trade Officer Grade owe much to Jimmy McGregor and Bill Dorward for their determination that common sense rather than establishment niceties should prevail in ensuring the department discharged its remit as regards Hong Kong's trade and industry. I remember that Kwun Tong and Junk Bay were once rejected sites for the territorial expansion that Hong Kong so desperately needed. Only relentless nagging from McGregor brought these to fruition. Dorward operated in a different way. He was an excellent speaker and did much in his role as Chief Trade Negotiator to gain support for Hong Kong's way of thinking among other developing countries and sympathy from those in developed countries who recognised their demands were unreasonable but as civil servants, had their own political masters to serve. Nor can the enormous contribution of two Administrative Officers in furthering the interests of the Trade Officer Grade be ignored— Philip Haddon-Cave himself, who was both staunch supporter of the essential role of the Trade Officer Grade and doughty opponent as he eventually achieved his goals. The other was David Jordan, who, as Head of DC&I, and later, of the Trade, Industry and Customs 'super-Department', would brook no interference whatsoever from anybody where he saw his department threatened. It might just have been coincidence that Haddon-Cave did not achieve his goals until well into the retirement of David Jordan. And when 'administrativisation' did finally come under considerable public debate, Jordan was one of the first to protest from six thousand miles away in Britain. Another aspect of the saga is that although the dispute lasted over twenty years, it did not become public knowledge until the year in which Haddon-Cave published his plans. This says much for both sides that there were more pressing and important public interest issues that had to be dealt with than petty establishment sensitivities. At no time can I recall an occasion when the intergrade rivalries between AOs and TOs affected the effective and efficient discharge of our mutual responsibilities in the field of trade and industry.

Eric Ho, in his book *Times of Change* (Hong Kong University Press, 2005) tells of his struggle within the government to gain acceptance for Chinese Administrative Officers. Our TOGA struggle was not on the basis of discrimination by country of origin — Chinese officers predominated by far in the Trade Officer Grade. Rather, it sought to force understanding that it lay in the best interests of Hong Kong that the government should maintain a cadre of officers who could bring years of considerable and, sometimes, bitter experience to bear on the problems that confronted the territory. The settlement of so many of these was made possible because over the years good relationships and indeed friendships had built up between the Hong Kong 'regulars' and their 'adversaries' in overseas administrations. I first met Ambassador Tran van Thinh of the EEC when he and I were juniors working on GSP. I first met the USA's Deputy Special Trade Representative, Ambassador Mike Smith, when I was the baggage boy on one our earlier negotiations and he was a minion in State Department. Arthur Dunkel was Switzerland's trade negotiator before he became Director General of the GATT. Mahmoud Hamza became a dear friend when he was Egypt's representative in Geneva and I was on the TSB. My long-standing relationship with John Beck of the European Commission established over many negotiations with the EEC made it possible for us to find a way to overcome seemingly irreconcilable positions in 1981 and 1982. This name-dropping is only to make the point that continuity was such an important aspect of securing the best possible deal on offer. Things could, possibly would, have been very different if a new Hong Kong face appeared at every negotiation because establishment rules required regular interdepartmental postings. Trust and understanding would have had to be built from scratch each time. An incident in Geneva illustrates the problem. The representatives of Singapore and of Malaysia and Hong Kong's Peter Tsao all bore a striking resemblance to each other. A newcomer to the trade scene mistakenly took Peter for the Singapore Ambassador. 'I regret I cannot agree with the claims put forward by Ambassador Tang', said the newcomer. A buzz went round the room, and the newcomer, realising his mistake, apologised. Peter Tsao was on his feet in a flash assuring the newcomer that he had been called names much worse than that.

To persuade us of the benefits of administrativisation, Philip Haddon-Cave took three of us, Bill Dorward, Peter Tsao and me, out to lunch. Peter, was by this time quite favourably disposed — he saw first Bill, and then me, next in line, blocking his path to the top trade job. Bill, already Director of Trade, Industry and Customs was content to stay there but had no objection to being moved upwards should the opportunity arise. Only I remained unconvinced. As the wine flowed, so the arguments against administrativisation seemed to me to become clearer. Philip was in full flow about the wonders of his new system. The discussion got quite heated. In 1980, I had had a battle with cancer which, thanks to a generous government and the skills of the Medical Department, I was able to conquer.

'Well, I'm glad it was Dr. Ho Hung Chiu and not an admin officer that was looking after me in 1980', I blurted out. Peter Tsao departed swiftly for the 'Gents'. Bill Dorward found something of absorbing interest on the ceiling, and Philip laughed uproariously. He later wrote me a warm personal thank-you letter on my retirement.

The big question is whether administrativisation was necessary and whether it worked. As an ex-civil servant, my answer to both questions is typically yes and no. I think it was right that TOGA should resist the moves for the ten to fifteen years that we did because this was a time when the defence of Hong Kong's manufacturing and trading interests was so important. By 1989, when I left Hong Kong, things were already changing. Reliance on manufacturing was declining and Hong Kong was becoming increasingly services-oriented. New problems of a different kind were beginning to emerge. For me, personally, I lived with Haddon-Cave's new system for about six months and realised it was not my bag. I was appointed Regional Secretary (Hong Kong and Kowloon) and became the Honourable Lawrence Mills with a seat on the Legislative Council. I found myself turning up on a Wednesday for LEGCO, and during the week, swearing in Boy Scouts, liaising with district boards and *kai fongs* (neighbourhood associations), going to dragon boat races with the Governor and telling people in stirring speeches that drugs were bad for them — I would have thought they knew that. I then had to report each month what the 'grass roots' were saying and thinking about the government and its policies, when a *gwai lo* was probably the last person they would tell, even if I could understand what they were saying. (I had had a three-month intensive Cantonese course.)[1] So, I decided to take early retirement and move on to other things.

Whether the government was better for administrativisation, I leave others to judge. What I can say is that many of those administrative officers who had

---

[1] In DC&I, we used to require a monthly report from our overseas offices. These were a chore and rarely served any purpose as we were in daily touch with them anyway. Our man in Washington made the point by writing one month 'In the period under review, your representative attended fourteen cocktail parties, unwittingly insulted a lady from the Eastern bloc (at least I assumed she was a lady as everyone called her Olga), trod on twenty-seven toes, and dropped three bricks ...' The practice was discontinued.

the benefit of spells in DC&I went on to bigger and better things. Donald Tsang has not done too badly. Or Anson Chan, or Akers-Jones, or Haddon-Cave, or Jack Cater, or Eric Ho, among others. Derek Jones, originally our man in Geneva, went on to fill three Secretary posts with distinction. As for the TOGA members who became 'generalists', the list is both long and impressive. Peter Tsao filled two Secretary posts, T. H. 'Brian' Chau two others, and many of the more junior ATOs and TOs went on to become Heads of Department. Michael Wu joined the Hong Kong Securities and Futures Commission and, later, moved on to Shanghai as Deputy Chairman of the Shanghai Stock Exchange. Justin Yue resigned from government altogether and became an industrialist and successful racehorse owner instead. John C. C. Chan ran Kowloon Motor Bus for many years and served both as Chairman of the Hong Kong Club and the Royal Hong Kong Jockey Club. Jimmy McGregor eventually finished up with a knighthood and a seat on EXCO. The only one in my view who got a raw deal was Bill Dorward, a supporter of administrativisation from the beginning. To make the system work he had to be removed from the post of Director of Trade, Industry and Customs. In Peter Principle terms, he was not promoted to his level of incompetence but given the lateral arabesque instead, and became Hong Kong Trade Commissioner, spending his final years with the government, in New York.

And, as for me, well, I do a little fishing off the end of Brighton pier and ponder the wonders of the Holy Koran. In 1990, I converted to Islam, found happiness and contentment and now keep myself busy recording the experiences of the time I spent in the Middle East in my second book, *Lawrence of Suburbia* ....

Epilogue

So, that is the story of my years in Hong Kong. It was a challenging time for the territory and an exciting period for me. I would not have wished to spend those years in any other place or in any other way. To my mind, I arrived at just the right time and I left at just the right time. The Hong Kong of 1958 was so different from that of 1989. Within those thirty-one years, Hong Kong was transformed from a dot on the map with its name underlined in red and the letters (Br.) after it, to a place of which everyone had heard, in which all had prospered, with an economic record that few, if any, have equalled. Yet, the reasons for its success contained no closely guarded secrets, the means were available to all; they were demonstrably successful; and almost universally ignored.

In struggling to describe adequately the basis for this transformation, I came across the last published article of the late Milton Friedman, the 1976 Nobel laureate in economics and senior research fellow at Stanford's Hoover Institution. In October 2006, he wrote:[1]

'At the end of World War II, Hong Kong was a dirt-poor island with a per capita income about one quarter that of Britain's. By 1997, when sovereignty was transferred to China, its per capita income was roughly equal to that of the departing colonial power, even though Britain had experienced sizeable growth over the same period. That was a striking demonstration of the productivity of freedom, of what people can do when they are left free to pursue their own interests.

'The success of *laissez-faire* in Hong Kong was a major factor in encouraging China and other countries to move away from centralized control toward greater reliance on private enterprise and the free market. As a result, they too have benefited from rapid economic growth. The ultimate fate of China

---

[1]   Milton Friedman, 'Hong Kong Wrong', *Wall Street Journal*, 6 October 2006, A14.

depends, I believe, on whether it continues to move in Hong Kong's direction faster than Hong Kong moves in China's.'

There is not much that can be added to that because anybody with the slightest knowledge of, or interest in, Hong Kong can see for themselves the truth it encapsulates.

What makes the Hong Kong story intriguing, as I have tried to show, is that in protecting 'the productivity of freedom, of what people can do when they are left free to pursue their own interests … and … the success of laissez-faire … and … reliance on private enterprise and the free market', Hong Kong had to engage in practices totally at variance with its fundamental philosophy.

This philosophy, attributed by most to the tenure of Sir John Cowperthwaite as Financial Secretary and described on a number of occasions by one of his successors, Sir Philip Haddon-Cave, as 'positive non-interventionism', could only be defended by means of Hong Kong engaging with those with different philosophies and greater economic and political power, and then fettering its ability to pursue the philosophy at the heart of its success, thereby, creating the paradox, the subject of this book.

The paradox was then compounded by the irony that the way in which Hong Kong went about playing the game by the rules of the other side, enshrined in such instruments as the GATT, the MFA, certification of origin and Commonwealth Preference, furthered the interests of Hong Kong immeasurably and those of the rule-makers, hardly at all. In so doing, Hong Kong created yet another phenomenon, what might be called 'negative positive-non-interventionism', that is to say, if positive non-intervention means a conscious decision to do nothing, then, negative positive-non-intervention, is the conscious decision to do just enough to preserve the ability to do nothing.

Mr. Friedman might be spinning in his grave at such a proposition; yet, Hong Kong did precisely that and has derived much of its prosperity from it.

By agreeing to trade restrictions, by limiting the activities of its greatest export earner, its largest industry and its highest employer of labour, as well as by the effective (= doing the right things) and efficient (= doing things right) way it exploited the constraints, Hong Kong not only survived, but prospered.

Is there then a lesson here for others? Is negative positive-non-intervention the answer to the world's ills? I think not. Negative positive-non-intervention was a product of its time, a time that has passed. So, we need to add one more word to our definition: Hong Kong deployed, in effect, *timely* negative positive-non-interventionism.

As I said in the Prologue, Hong Kong has always had to accept and adapt to the circumstances in which it found itself at any particular time. By 1989, a change in the structure of Hong Kong's economy was already underway. It had moved from entrepôt immediately after the Second World War to manufacturing centre in the 1960s and 1970s. Then, with growing offshore investments engendered by textile restraints and the opening up of China, servicing those investments became increasingly important. Hong Kong was changing into the front office for China's massive expansion. The service industries saw the benefits of Hong Kong's open economy and business-friendly environment. Hong Kong no longer offered 'prices lower than in their country of origin' as one of the old slogans of the Hong Kong Tourist Association used to claim. According to a popular saw of the time, Chinese *amahs*, now replaced by Filipina maids, owned the properties they had once worked in. Hong Kong had become prosperous.

As this history makes clear, the MFA changed many things in Hong Kong. One can never say whether this was for the best since no one knows what might have been. It is a fact, however, that Hong Kong profited mightily from the restraints on its trade thanks to its ability to exploit them to the full. With advice directly from the TEXTAB, Hong Kong's negotiators were able to find solutions to, and squeeze the last drop from, seemingly unredeemable situations. Hong Kong's huge quota base created a massive sellers' market. When a Hong Kong manufacturer could not fill an order, he was off to the Philippines or Sri Lanka where he would open a factory and deliver the goods from there. He was able to charge buyers the highest price the market would stand, inflated by the premium that the quota transfer system provided. The wealth thus created was ploughed back into Hong Kong or invested in other countries in the region. Huge investments were made in China, thus recementing original ties and building understanding in China as to how valuable Hong Kong really was.

This prosperity flowed downwards to the whole population. Other parts of the government came into their own as high revenues from low taxes and income from land sales financed more social and public works projects.

Hong Kong achieved all of this alone, while it relied on market forces (even those involving restraints on trade) to lead it where best it should go.

So, when, within a few years more, Hong Kong no longer stood as the industrial heart of South East Asia and had transmogrified, yet again, into something different, this time, to take its place among the world's leading service and financial centres, one could be forgiven for thinking that all the effort that went into preserving Hong Kong industry, all the crises that it had faced and dealt with, all the indignities forced upon Hong Kong by those with greater political and economic power and all the grandstanding, as erstwhile Financial Secretary Bembridge called it, went for naught.

Nonetheless, the older hands might justly claim that it all started with just five pieces of paper and TEXTAB meetings on a Thursday afternoon in Fire Brigade Building.

Index

For convenience, the principal provisions of instruments such as the GATT and MFA are indexed under the headings GATT principal provisions, MFA principal provisions, and so on followed by page references. Other references to the GATT, etc, are listed in the usual way.

Individual persons are grouped under the generic heading Personalities.

Given the various name changes undergone by the (original) European Economic Community, all references to the group are placed under the heading EEC.

DATE DUE

DEC 1 6 2019	